Love & light.

Chris Smith..

Urban Science Education for the Hip-hop Generation

CULTURAL PERSPECTIVES IN SCIENCE EDUCATION: RESEARCH DIALOGS 01

Series editor
Kenneth Tobin, *The Graduate Center, City University of New York, USA*
Catherine Milne, *Steinhardt School o Culture, Education, and Human Development, New York University*

Scope
Research dialogs consists of books written for undergraduate and graduate students of science education, teachers, parents, policy makers, and the public at large. Research dialogs bridge theory, research, and the practice of science education. Books in the series focus on what we know about key topics in science education – including, teaching, connecting the learning of science to the culture of students, emotions and the learning of science, labs, field trips, involving parents, science and everyday life, scientific literacy, including the latest technologies to facilitate science learning, expanding the roles of students, after school programs, museums and science, doing dissections, etc.

Urban Science Education for the Hip-hop Generation

Christopher Emdin
Teachers College, Columbia University

SENSE PUBLISHERS
ROTTERDAM/BOSTON/TAIPEI

A C.I.P. record for this book is available from the Library of Congress.

ISBN: 978-90-8790-986-4 (paperback)
ISBN: 978-90-8790-987-1 (hardback)
ISBN: 978-90-8790-988-8 (e-book)

Published by: Sense Publishers,
P.O. Box 21858, 3001 AW
3001 AW Rotterdam
Rotterdam, The Netherlands
http://www.sensepublishers.com

Printed on acid-free paper

For Monique Eniola Emdin

TABLE OF CONTENTS

FOREWORD

I must begin by saying that as a philosopher affected by existentialism, phenomenology, critical theory, and aesthetics, I've spent much time combating positivism when applied to values or the arts. I have labored over a foreword with the hope of being true to my commitments and beliefs—and reading this fine work through a lens that would not distort or would not be too slanted in my direction.

I thought I could write that I had just been introduced to a new verbal and gestural language shared by certain underprivileged youth but not understood by their teachers who mistakenly categorized all poor city youth as "urban youth" without distinguishing them from hip-hop youth. I see how that meant a lack of understanding of numbers of such young people in science classes.

Surely the reader is familiar with the many books about the misunderstandings and the stereotyping of urban youth as resistant to savage inequality. Troubled as we all are by prescribed curricula and their imposition on kids. I don't really know alternatives in science education, I know Kuhn's work and others—and I would turn to Dewey and Schon. Here, I turn to this work.

As a teacher educator largely in the Deweyan tradition, I have thought of education as an expansion and deepening of educative experiences, those which feed into and make understandable the 'doings and undergoings' that mark the processes of becoming. Becoming, or coming into consciousness, is the enactment of the ability to think about and reflect on oneself. For the educator, it is the opening up of the space to find out the purpose of teaching; which in the Deweyan tradition is rooted in considering and valuing students' experiences. A concern for beginning and engaging with students' experiences has always been of the first importance. This is why I welcome this thoughtful and eye-opening introduction to hip-hop and join Christopher Emdin in pushing for the realization that we are far too prone to stereotype and categorize urban youth today without some knowledge of the way many of them have learned the values and expressiveness intrinsic to hip-hop.

For teachers willing to attend to what to them may be a generally unfamiliar gestural and verbal language, an expansion of their experience awaits. Through this work, the process of becoming (in this case becoming an urban science educator) begins. Even as bilinguality and multilinguality may open new logics and perspectives without eroding a native language, so may hip-hop open new pathways to communication among urban girls and boys. Meanings are created when people are able to translate their gains and losses, their feelings, angers, hopes, and disappointments into words that they know those they are addressing will comprehend. The same is true when it comes to gestures, body movements, swaggering walks, and even dances, which so many members of the dominant culture either have forgotten or never knew.

Despite the ignorance or purposeful dismissal of hip-hop and its words, gestures, and body movements by the dominant culture, many of us have come to understand that emotions that are inexpressible in ordinary language can find expression in movement. We have only to recall tango, flamenco, and the many folk and circle dances linked to mourning and celebration; and the proud or cocky or defiant walk of many city young people will come clear. It may well be that certain teachers of these youngsters have had painful experiences of their own in their early lives, but have felt compelled to repress them in order to speak the supposedly standard language of the system. But we might also recollect the painful youth of someone like Frank McCourt, who emerged from the slums of Ireland to become in time a remarkable teacher in New York. And lately, we have read the books of younger activist teachers who have somehow tuned into the hard lives of their students and turned out to receive good grades from the authorities. None of this, however, takes away from the important viewing Christopher Emdin provides on the dialogues and understandings achieved by the hip-hop generation, not to speak of the work they do, somehow to infuse neglected, sometimes violent neighborhoods with the vibrant and strangely knightly spirit of hip-hop.

Maxine Greene

Professor Emeritus, Teachers College, Columbia University
Philosopher in Residence, Lincoln Center Institute for the Arts in Education

INTRODUCTION

Imagine if you could spend every second of the next three years in an institution that values who you are, embraces where you come from, and teaches what has been described as the most challenging subject matter in a way that is engaging, respectful of your culture, and aligned to the way that you see the world. The feelings that would be generated from that experience would be able to propel you into new possibilities for your future. You might be convinced that what has been previously presented as challenging, is really not anything out of your intellectual reach. Your confidence would grow, your faith in your academic abilities would develop, and over time, you would begin to see that you have the tools to be successful at whatever task is set in front of you.

Considering the length of the typical school day, the time that an average student spends in school, and the years of schooling from kindergarten to high school, I have calculated that the average student spends the equivalent of three full years (without interruption) inside a classroom. This is more than enough time to foster experiences in school that (strive to) bring out the greatness/potential inherent within each and every student. Given the time that educators have with students, they should be able to easily spark an interest in school and schooling, and develop in students an unquenchable passion for challenging subjects like science.

Unfortunately, the time that is spent in schools can also very easily be the root for disinterest in school, disdain for teachers, and an alienation from subject areas that are taught without a consideration for the cultural knowledge that students bring to the classroom. Whether classrooms are a bevy of positive experiences that foster interest in school, or negative experiences that push students away from school is dependent upon the structure of the classroom, and the nature of instruction - which are both affected by teachers' exposure to, and comfort with, the culture of their students.

In urban classrooms, the culture of the school is generally different from the culture of its students. In addition, a majority of students are either African American or Latino/a while their teachers are mostly White. Culturally, urban youth are mostly immersed in a generally communal and distinctly hip-hop based way of knowing and being. By this, I mean that the shared realities that come with being from socioeconomically deprived areas brings urban youth together in ways that transcend race/ethnicity and embraces their collective connections to hip-hop. Concurrently, hip-hop is falsely interpreted as being counter to the objectives of school, or seen as "outside of" school culture.

Culture is the summation of the beliefs and practices that a particular group of people holds (Bourdieu, 1993). More specifically, it is the sum of the schema and practices expressed through the shared meanings of symbols that allow people to communicate with each other (Geertz, 1973).

The urban science classroom holds multiple cultures that inform perceptions of, and goals for, the classroom. These cultures can be grouped into four categories: the culture of science, the culture of urban teaching, the culture of urban students, and the culture of the urban teacher. In science, there are distinct beliefs and symbols that members of a community use in their manifold investigations and communications with each other. For example, science formulas are made up of letters that signify words and symbols that only those who are embedded in science understand. Therefore, there is a distinct culture of science. Urban teaching also has its own culture, which is grounded in the historically rooted, and commonly accepted, belief that socioeconomically deprived urban youth and students of color require strong "classroom management," hyper-structured classroom environments, and teaching that assimilates students into an established world of school. Urban students have their own culture, which is the summation of the beliefs and practices of the students' out of school experiences as they become manifested in classrooms. Finally, urban teachers have their own culture, which is a summation of the beliefs and practices of the teacher and the ways that these phenomena combine to create who the teacher becomes in the classroom. This last type of culture (the teacher's culture) is most significant because if it becomes amenable to change, it can allow the established culture of science and the manifest needs and identities of urban youth to come together. When these categories come together in synergistic ways, I argue that teaching can be more successful.

As more students enter into urban schools, and the teacher workforce increasingly does not reflect the culture of students, divisions between student and teacher increase accordingly. Statistics tell us that the enrollment of minority students in K-12 public schools in the United States has increased dramatically from 22 percent in 1972 to 43 percent in 2006 (NCES, 2008). By the year 2050, "the nation's population of children is expected to be 62 percent minority-(U.S. Census Bureau News, 2008). Recent research tells us that while the minority enrollment in public schools is increasing, and students are more and more engaged in hip-hop (Stoval, 2006), science and mathematics achievement of Black and Latino/a students is decreasing (Brand, Glasson, & Green, 2006; CGS, 2008). researchers also tell us that a large number of failing students are concentrated in urban schools that are disproportionally populated with Black and Latino/a students and teachers from ethnic and racial backgrounds other than those of students (Lankford, Loeb, & Wycoff, 2002; Sleeter, 2001).

The underlying premise of this work is not that the racial and ethnic differences between students and teachers in urban settings is the cause for low student achievement in science. The point is that effective teaching in urban science classrooms must consider both a deep understanding of subject matter and a profound understanding of the cultural backgrounds of students of color in urban settings (Fusco, 2001; Lee & Fradd, 1998). Therefore, I move forward in this work with the belief that a consideration of the cultural differences between students and teachers is absolutely necessary, and that the embracement of hip-hop can be used as a means to bridge these breaches.

While other educators/researchers have identified the importance of a focus on student culture, they have not recognized the significance of hip-hop culture. While they have focused on hip-hop as music and text, they generally have not considered that it undergirds the existence of urban youth in more complex ways (Hill, 2009).

In addition, they have not considered the ways that hip-hop specifically relates to science, which is the subject that urban students are most marginalized from.

The statistics and underlying themes stated above provide insight into the work that will come in this book. While I do critique the work of teachers and researchers, this is not a body of work that is intended to attack teachers or researchers. I believe that researchers are fundamentally good-hearted and want to address the achievement gaps that plague urban schools. I also believe that teachers are important for student learning, and in most cases, they teach because they want to meet the needs of their students. However, there is great variation in effectiveness across teachers (Kane, Rockoff & Staiger, 2006; Rivkin, Hanushek & Kain, 2005; Rockoff, 2004), and researchers are often ignorant of the nuances of student culture (Emdin & Lehner, 2007).

Science education programs across the country have identified that many teachers are not effective because of their lack of knowledge of student culture. In response, they have begun to address issues related to the culture of urban youth of color by offering/requiring classes in multicultural education, and holding seminars that address student culture and science. In one instance, the coordinator of a science education program I had a conversation with mentioned that he has begun to script lessons and provide a step-by-step protocol that he thinks will assist in the delivery of science content to urban youth.

Unfortunately, these attempts to address the needs of urban science teachers fail to recognize that a mere introduction to multicultural education will not necessarily provide the deeper insights into student culture that teachers need to succeed (McAllister & Irvine, 2000). These attempts will, and have failed due in part to an inadequate focus on significant yet under discussed issues like interactions between students and teachers and the absence of a focus on hip-hop culture.

This work purposefully avoids providing scripts or step-by-step processes like those that science education programs and many quick fix professional development programs found in urban schools provide. Its purpose is to introduce urban education, and science education in particular, to the larger issues related to the culture of urban youth and science instruction. Its chief function is to inform teachers on how to reach hip-hop youth by immersing the reader in the larger ways of thinking and challenging their existent practice, and providing them with insight into personal experiences related to hip-hop and science pedagogy that they would not have otherwise. I argue that providing teachers with this larger grounding, and then allowing them to create practical steps on their own challenges them to enact new means of connecting with hip-hop youth, and is in the spirit of the imagination and creativity inherent in hip-hop. The work is purposefully guided by the age old adage that says "Give a man a fish; you have fed him for today. Teach a man to fish; and you have fed him for a lifetime." I implore the reader who is accustomed to the status quo in science teaching and learning to be open minded and soak in the work, and then use it to effectively teach and research hip-hop youth for a lifetime.

ON RAP AND HIP-HOP

An overview of, and grounding in, the culture

Neither hip-hop nor science are new phenomena. They are each ways of looking at, and making sense of the world that can be traced to our earliest collective histories as human beings. As long as man has walked the earth, there have been questions about the world, theories about how we arrived on this planet, and studies of our immediate and distant surroundings. This deep questioning, and the search for more information about our surroundings are the building blocks of science. Therefore, it is fair to say that science has always been a part of the human experience.

At the same time, human beings have also had a collective history of not valuing difference. We ostracize those who we perceive as outside of established norms, and subjugate those who we see as weaker than us, or a threat to our sameness. Consequently, there have always been groups of people who have been treated uncivilly, shunned for their beliefs, and who in response, develop ways of looking at the world that are outside of the norm. While these ways of looking at the world are unfamiliar to most people, many others who have also been treated unfairly understand them. Take for example the popular science story of Galileo and his detention for the sake of his societally unaccepted scientific writings in 1633. Then consider rap group NWA and the harsh critique its members endured for the sake of their raps about their take on life in Los Angeles, California in 1988. In each case, Galileo and NWA questioned the way life was, used an artifact like writing or rapping to buck against established norms, were punished for doing so, and eventually caught the attention of others who identified with them because of their anti-establishment positions.

In the case of hip-hop and its chief artifact - rap, their birth in the United States during the 1970's marks the advent of new forms of expression for people who have been oppressed since the beginning of time. Hip-hop culture is rooted in West African traditional music that has blended percussion from talking drums with songs of religious worship and celebration for centuries. Rap is found in African-American storytelling and singing about the tribulations of slavery prior to, and after the abolishment of slavery in 1865, and forms of both hip-hop and rap can be traced to the Caribbean art of toasting and dee-jaying on the island of Jamaica in the 1950's.

Hip-hop's roots in rhythm and storytelling despite the pain and anguish its ancestors have dealt with resounds with urban youth, and allows rap to evolve into the main avenue of voice for urban marginalized youth across the globe. These roots have led hip-hop culture to become the once secret and now public, yet unheralded path through which urban youth share their experiences with those who have a similar plight.

In the Bronx, New York, in the 1970s, those who inhabited the lowest socioeconomic spaces struggled to find a way to provide voice to each other (Neal, 1999) and merged the art of speaking over beats with rhythm and rhyme (rap) with unique forms of dance (break-dancing) and distinctly urban visual art (graffiti) to express their view of the world. Since then, hip-hop has emerged to become not only a form of expression, but the culture of urban socioeconomically deprived youth and those who identify with them.

Focusing on Rap

As mentioned earlier, rap music is the chief artifact of hip-hop and is one of the purest expressions of urban African American and Latino/a youth culture. It creates scenarios where intensely personal words and ideas that an individual holds get introduced to others in ways that are unique enough to be personal, yet distinct enough to ring true to listeners across demographics and generations. Once again, this distinctness exists because rap music has its roots in aspects of Black culture and tradition like Negro spirituals and spoken word poetry, and hip-hop music is a coagulation of centuries of practices, rules and traditions (Ramsey, 2003).

Since, "Black music has always been a primary means of cultural expression for African Americans, particularly during especially difficult social periods and traditions" (Rose, 1994, p. 184), the feeling of living in a seemingly eternal difficult social life for minoritized youth calls for the rise of a medium that expresses the realities of their lives. Rap music is the text produced by those who are involved in hip-hop, and is a medium through which the culture of the marginalized is expressed. Rap's antecedents in the traditions of the Black experience in the United States, leads to its ability to provide descriptions of contemporary urban life in oppressive social spheres beyond the U.S. This causes it to display a quality that transcends space and time while it reflects the experiences of those within a current and specific context. This attribute of rap is closely related to the chronotypic nature of certain literary texts that express an "intrinsic connectedness of temporal and spatial relationships that are artistically expressed in literature" (Bakhtin, 1981 p. 84). Rap music becomes the literature of marginalized people whose backgrounds are rooted in oral traditions. It connects their histories, echoes their pain, and concurrently articulates the stance of new people who have been, or are being, marginalized in different spaces around the globe. It is the verbal expression of the realities of social actors in contexts where they are either not allowed to fully participate or cannot be heard because their histories, traditions, and voices are different from those of a dominant group. Therefore, it is amenable to being, and often becomes a reflection of the experiences of urban youth when they have been silenced within schools.

The first time that many people outside of New York City heard of rap or hip-hop, it was through the song "Rappers Delight" by the Sugar Hill Gang. The song received widespread commercial exposure as simple lyrics that showed bravado and celebration were rapped over an already popular disco song instrumental. The attention that the song received introduced many people to the infectious genre of hip-hop music.

Despite the historic significance of Rappers Delight to hip-hop culture, the power of hip-hop's descriptive and vivid imagery was not displayed via song until three years later. In 1982, a record by Melle-Mel entitled "The Message" gave insight into how rap music became the voice of a new generation, and showed the potential of hip-hop to give insight to the experiences of urban youth. The song described life in the inner city and painted a vivid picture of the streets of New York. One of the main lyrics to this song, "It's like a jungle some times it makes me wonder, how I keep from going under" (Melle-Mel, 1982) gave a glimpse into not just the physical realities of life in the inner city but also the emotional frustration that accompanies the life of participants in hip-hop. This song serves as an example of the dialectical relationship between rap and the inner city where the streets speak to the music and the music retells the message received from the streets. Artists rap about the struggles of living in urban settings and speak directly to people who are on the streets experiencing the same thing. This type of rap, in which the focus is on lived experience that consumers of the music can identify with through their own experiences, is a significant part of hip-hop where the streets and the music become single entities that cannot be separated from each other.

As hip-hop's voice traveled from its humble beginnings in the Bronx to other boroughs of New York City, and the world, it continued to tell tales of the struggles of life in the inner city and celebrated its uniqueness from other forms of music. The fact that it had become something that was owned by those furthest from the mainstream or traditionally considered as outside of the norm became a key part of the music, much of which was originally produced on the front steps and in the cafeterias of New York City public schools. The fact that the creators of hip-hop were urban public school students who felt like they were not a part of the establishment in school or in the world is an under-focused upon component of the history of hip-hop. This fact leads to two distinct ideas that undergird the work in this book. Firstly, hip-hop is owned and spawned by marginalized voices. Secondly, because it is mostly created by urban youth, it provides insight into the inner-workings of their thoughts about the world, and consequently, is a tool for unlocking their academic potential.

Those who are most marginalized within the social fields they inhabit hold on dearly to hip-hop and rap, even as it goes through eras/phases where its main focus is celebration, subtle commercialism, overt materialism, increased socio-political commentary, and gross commercialism. As hip-hop goes through these phases, it always expresses some part of the lives of its participants at a particular point in time. The phases of hip-hop within the United States are marked by changes in the conditions of the inner cities throughout the country. Eras like the gangster rap (a response to police violence and socioeconomic depression) or self-conscious era (a response to increasing visibility of Black scholars and intellectuals) in hip-hop mirror what was occurring on the socio-political landscape of the country and their implications on the urban populace. The music was interpreting what urban youth

3

were feeling, and what urban youth are feeling, dictates the ways that they should be taught.

As outlined earlier, rap music has consistently translated the voices of the socio-economically disadvantaged within the inner city to others who share their plight. In modern hip-hop, where the music of the culture has been marketed and commercialized, voices from urban settings have been exposed to the world. Many believe this large-scale commercialization of hip-hop has resulted in the pollution of the true voices of urban youth and an over-saturation of negative parts of the culture that record companies choose to present to the world. However, rap music still, through students' voices, provides insider perspectives on schools. Therefore, anyone interested in bettering the conditions of students who have been marginalized from achievement within formal institutions of learning must listen to and learn from hip-hop.

The Fallacy in "Hip Hop is Dead"

While many entities who financially profit from the commercialization of rap music lament its supposed demise because of declining record sales, hip-hop purists lament the high number of commercially successful rap artists who seem to only show a superficial involvement in the true essence of the culture. These contrasting views about the state of hip-hop lead to a questioning of the viability of hip-hop. They also open up a discussion about what really is hip-hop. In my quest to spark this discussion, I have posed many questions about hip-hop to students who describe themselves as hip-hop youth. My work with this population uncovers that they perceive hip-hop to be the combination of their realities and experiences, which is sometimes expressed as music, but also goes beyond it. In essence, urban youth see hip-hop as not just a musical genre, but as their culture.

While the notion of hip-hop as culture will be elaborated further on in this work, it is important at this stage to recognize that interacting with urban African American and Latino/a youth whose parents and grand-parents created hip-hop in the 1970's, shows that the culture is still a deep part of urbanness (a state of being urban) about 40 years after its "birth." In fact, as urban youth I work with consume and create rap music, they complain about the development of a false type of hip-hop (commercialized rap) that does not truly reflect their culture. They clearly demarcate the lines between rap music they listen to because it sounds good, and true hip-hop music that is true to their culture. I make this point to lay the foundation for an understanding amongst readers that when hip-hop is being discussed, existent messages about its demise relate more specifically to the overshadowing of certain parts of hip-hop by commercial rap. The true culture and spirit of hip-hop is still alive. In fact, even at points where commercial hip-hop appears to be at its height, artists who are in touch with the core of hip-hop culture critique its commercial forms and argue that true hip-hop is still alive and strong. Artists like the Roots (1996) have consistently responded to the commodification of hip-hop culture by explaining that despite the fact that "the true elements of hip-hop have been forsaken, [and] now its all contractual and about money making," hip-hop remains a space where "world populations, address their frustration."

For teachers and researchers who intend to work with students who identify themselves as part of hip-hop culture, it is necessary to constantly keep in mind that what is perceived as the death of hip-hop is actually an increased visibility of commercialized or false hip-hop that causes a masking of the core of the culture. Williams (1991) describes a process where certain people take an individual's reality (which is what hip-hop is) and places it into a process that "puts reality up for sale and makes meaning fungible: dishonest, empty, irresponsible" (p. 30). This has been the case with hip-hop culture, where its most unattractive aspects are presented as the face of the culture. For example, at any given time, there are forms of hip-hop music being created that portray everything from violence and misogyny to love, self-awareness and political activism. However, commercial forms of hip-hop music that are produced for the masses who are not embedded in hip-hop culture often ignore the more positive forms of hip-hop and focus on easily sensationalized negative forms. I argue that the proliferation of these negative forms of hip-hop leads to the perpetuation of the grossly inaccurate myths that begin with the belief that urban youth embody all of the negative stereotypes that are associated with the commercial hip-hop music that is heard on the radio.

While I do not support or condone the gratuitously violent or hateful lyrics that are in some rap lyrics, it is important to recognize that these lyrics only provide a thin slice of hip-hop and an even thinner slice of hip-hop culture. Even the type of hip-hop music that is most often critiqued for negative lyrics (gangster rap) is merely a strand of rap music that is either inspired by the experiences of urban youth or a retelling of the artists experiences. A narrow view of hip-hop culture that does not recognize that participants in the culture who are rappers are describing truths in their experiences and those of their peers is flawed (Watkins, 2005). Furthermore, the lack of an understanding that rap, like literature, explores everything from reality and fantasy to fiction and non-fiction leads to an unjustifiably harsh critique of the culture and limits its potential as a teaching tool to "what not to do."

Students who are a part of hip-hop feel the effects of the negative ways they and their culture are portrayed and perceived. I argue that these feelings affect their abilities to connect to the classroom and alienate them from a field of study like science, which is taught in ways that run counter to hip-hop. Students in my research have discussed the ways that teachers perceive them and have made statements like "They (teachers) don't know about us and ...they don't care about what we say, they don't listen to us... (and they) they don't listen to rap." Rap artists share similar sentiments as the students and speak to and about science educators and researchers in statements like "he wants to be an astronaut and fly to space, but his teachers told him that he just ain't got what it takes" (Jay Electronica, 2008). These words by urban youth and hip-hop artists demonstrate an insight into schooling that scholars and educators are unaware of. It reveals that "the hip-hop underground is the most socially and politically active generation since the long death and silence of the Black community which fell asleep in the 1980s" (Banfield,

2004 p. 203), and as such, it tells educators that the insight that urban hip-hop youth provide need to be heard, and utilized to improve the state of urban education.

Currently, the connections discussed above have not been made. In fact, the lines of division between hip-hop and education are often created by academics, politicians, and teachers, and are reinforced by the curricula within urban schools. Within schools, student interest and the absence of connections between hip-hop and education are rarely explored beyond complaints about hip-hop youth's disinterest in school. This stance does not consider that student complaints, rap songs and lyrics that appear to denounce school and education are merely reflections of the frustration students experience in schools. Rather than look at hip-hop music as anti-school, I suggest we view them as rapper Common (1997) does and see them as "smoke signals" that establish a relationship between urban communities and the rapper, and that gives the rapper the authority to speak for urban youth and share their passions. Therefore, if we are hearing negative lyrics about school, law enforcement or any other phenomena in urban settings, it is often because there are issues within the street, neighborhood or school that are being signalled. The rap artist's message is a reflection of the hip-hop participants' experiences. Lyrics about schools (whether negative or positive) exist because urban youth have an interest in being successful within schools. Hip-hop's critiques about the injustices in the world exist because somewhere in the world, someone is using rap to let off a smoke signal to alert the world that an issue has to be addressed.

Alive and Global: The Current State of Hip-hop

As a result of the wide distribution of hip-hop across the globe, and the ways that it speaks to populations that are marginalized from the socio-economic norms in places that traditionally would not be exposed to U.S. hip-hop music or culture, the emergence of indigenous and grassroots hip-hop among many traditionally marginalized populations (from New Zealand to New Guinea) has emerged. Hip-hop has grown to include many different national cultures, making it important to recognize that it has become a unified culture that informs multiple generations across various physical and symbolic boundaries. The fact that hip-hop is the unified language that many diverse populations share means that it must play a part in how these populations are educated. Only when a path to this understanding is cleared can we juxtapose analyses of urban schools, hip-hop, and science education to discover ways that these supposedly separate entities can coexist to develop a more effective vision of urban science education.

In order for a hip-hop based urban science education to exist, it is necessary to discover what is at the core of the culture of urban schools, hip-hop, and science education. It is only when this happens that the science education community can effectively begin to work towards situating hip-hop, school, and science within each other. It is only at this point that the maintenance of the status quo in regards to the growing numbers of students in urban areas who are disinterested in science can finally be addressed.

TEACH A NEW WAY

Wake up everybody no more sleepin' in bed
No more backward thinkin' time for thinkin' ahead
The world has changed so very much from what it used to be
There is so much hatred war and poverty
Wake up all the teachers time to teach a new way
Maybe then they'll listen to what you have to say
Cause they're the ones who's coming up and the world is in their hands
When you teach the children teach em the very best you can.

The world won't get no better if we just let it be
The world won't get no better we gotta change it yeah, just you and me.

Harold Melvin and the Blue Notes 1975

As I begin to address teaching in urban schools, some will see the arguments that I make as controversial. For others, they will either be an affirmation of what is already known, a clarification of issues they may have seen or experienced, or a chance to gain insight on issues they may have been unable or unwilling to explore. My intent is for the work to serve as an uncovering of truths that have been obscured and a means through which the reader is ushered into a new way of looking at the teaching and learning of students of color, particularly in science, within urban classrooms. My goals are simple. They are to invite audiences from varying ideological and theoretical backgrounds and perspectives to become students of hip-hop. In addition, I want the reader to work with me to understand the influence of hip-hop on the life experiences of students in the urban classroom. Finally, I want the reader to see hip-hop as a part of science teaching and learning and vice versa.

I embark on the task to meet the above-stated goals by nesting this work primarily in my own research and experiences within urban public schools. I believe that by sharing the tools I have crafted and discovered through my journey in urban science education, I will open up my world to the reader and provide the type of insight into urban science teaching and learning that can only be provided by the type of research I have conducted and the anecdotes that came from my experiences in urban science classrooms. I share my experiences as student, teacher, administrator and researcher, and pick apart my experiences in order to deconstruct the way urban classrooms were when I was a student, uncover the way that they are, and guide a path towards how they should be.

This work is the manifestation of thoughts about, and insight into, my experiences with urban schooling. It is also a guide for the use of tools I have both crafted and discovered on my journey in urban education. As the chapters progress, envision them as the carving out of holes in concrete walls that stand in the way to a path towards transforming the experiences of urban youth in classrooms. Each thought, and the suggestions they provoke, are a challenge to the existent power structures in urban education that inhibit teachers and researchers from understanding that conventional approaches to instruction in urban classrooms are not working and are long overdue for an overhaul. Each story, each sentence, each line, and each word is intended to be another tool for tearing down the walls that block us from our path. I focus specifically on the urban science classroom because it is the space where I have felt most marginalized from attainment in my youth and find the most challenge as a researcher. In this work, science and science education serve as both foci for the study, and tools for radical change in existing practices in urban schools. What I argue for in this work is the need for a means to teaching students in ways that meet their interests and ignite their passions. The work is a manifestation of a thought I have had since I was a student in a 7th grade classroom in Brooklyn, New York. Teachers have to teach a new way.

The first time I realized that someone else in the world thought there was a need to teach a new way, I was about thirteen years old. The day this revelation came, I was engaged in one of my favorite activities when my parents weren't home. I would cracked open a huge cardboard box that held my father's record collection, grab a stack of records, and lose myself in the artwork on the album covers. I would leaf through the 12 inch by 12 inch square covers of the albums for hours until I found a cover that caught my interest. When that happened, I would flip the album cover upside down, carefully watch the black vinyl slip through the cover and into my fingers, and guide it to an old record player in the back of the room so I could listen to what the artists had to offer.

Most often, the vivid colors of a funk album would catch my attention. I would play the record, let the bass driven melodies ooze through the speaker, and recite raps that I had crafted over the beats and melodies of songs created before my time. Sometimes, I would imitate hip-hop deejays and spin the records backwards when a break beat came in so I could hear a special part of the record over again. On occasion, I would fall in love with a song and play it for hours until I knew that my father was on his way home from work. I would then return the records to their rightful place, wonder in their ability to bring me to a place beyond the four walls of a Brooklyn apartment, and spend the rest of the day with a song or two dancing in my head.

On one particular day, as I sifted through a stack of records that all happened to have vivid colors and intricate artwork, one album cover struck me. Its color was a dull shade of green and it showed a landscape of mountains with one standing in front of the rest. The mountain that was out front was shaped like a Black man with an Afro. From the forehead of this mountain, a yellow flower grew and provided the only color to the otherwise dull cover. I was intrigued by the cover, pulled the album from its jacket, walked it to the record player, and dropped the needle on the title track. A piano riff played, the lyrics began, and after a challenge for the world to wake up, the words that opened up this chapter joined a barrage of blows that struck me.

The first blow was a line in the song about "hatred, war, and poverty." It immediately opened my eyes to the fact that issues that were relevant in my life in the 1990's were just as prevalent in 1975. As I reeled from that line, there was a lyric that called for teachers to "teach a new way" that struck just as hard, and etched itself into my subconscious. These words were what I wanted to say to my teachers as I wrestled with being stereotyped and feeling invisibile as a student in high school, college, and even graduate school.

The words "maybe then they'll listen to what you have to say" followed the request for teachers to teach a new way and provide a justification for, or reasoning behind the need to teach a new way. While this call to teach a new way is the underlying theme for this work, the reason behind why it is important to do so is the springboard from which the work is set in motion. I argue that the acknowledgment that a change in teaching practices may cause students to listen to a teacher when they normally would not, is an indication of the awareness that for many students, their disinterest or lack of success in school is a conscious decision. It is not that certain students cannot listen or cannot succeed. Rather, it is that they choose not to.

While this choice to not listen to the teacher may evolve into the enactment of unconscious practices that do not support school success, at its core, the decision is rooted in whether the student holds any value for the teacher or if the teacher's practices reflect a "new way" of teaching. I argue that the decision to not listen is a conscious effort to subvert the teacher's power and is a direct response to approaches to instruction that do not reflect what the student needs to connect to the classroom. This is particularly the case in science; where the ways that the subject has been taught, and even what is taught, has not changed much since the call to teach a new way was made years before I was born, and when the songs was released in the mid 1970s. The reality is that the emphasis in most science instruction is on helping students acquire what has come to be accepted as a fundamental base of scientific knowledge (Gallagher, 2000). Unfortunately, this limited focus on what is taught is accompanied by a strong focus on drilling in this fundamental information. Consequently, efforts to teach a new way have never been truly implemented on a broad enough scale to be acknowledged beyond individual cases, or enough for their true value to be determined.

THE RESULTS OF NOT TEACHING A NEW WAY

Much research has indicated that the nature of teaching in urban schools focuses more on classroom management and keeping students in line than on connecting them to an academic discipline (Darling-Hammond, 1997, Emdin, 2009). In classes where rigidity in the instruction takes preeminence over connecting students to an academic discipline, the classroom is viewed by urban youth as constraining. This is the case because within these classrooms, freedom to think beyond the instruction that is provided, or even to question what is being presented, is not allowed. For the secondary school students that I have taught, I find that those who have spent a majority of their lives within urban public schools find no need to move beyond the constraints of a closed, simple, and confining school system. For them, it is easier to play a prescribed role in the way that schooling is than it is to exert the energy to change it. Their experiences within schools, and their consequent perceptions of school, stand in sharp contrast to the fact that they are immersed in a culture outside of school that is rooted in breaking from constraints. Outside of school, they are welcomed into a community where they are lauded for thinking critically, and acclaimed for forging new paths of inquiry. This dynamic – of being constrained in one world and being free to move beyond constraints in another supports an aggressive move towards positioning oneself as beyond the trivialities of school. School is perceived as too simple and too prescribed. There is no new way.

In my work, I find that for members of the hip-hop community, the choice to become disinterested in what is going on in the classroom, or to not listen to the teacher, is a function of how trivial they think the classroom is, and the fact that they perceive they are superior to even an academically challenging class. In conversations with these students, they neither refer to a fear of, or an inability to engage in academic work, nor do they mention a fear of acting White. Rather, they speak about their strengths, the weaknesses of their school, and the inabilities of their teachers to be effective. Conversations with students who are part of hip-hop reveal that they understand that their lack of success in school "doesn't mean that I (they) couldn't be a doctor or a dentist" (Dead Prez, 2000). As one of my students mentioned, when he was queried about why he did not complete a lab report, "I don't do your work because I don't want to do your work. If it was my work, I would do it."

The typical teacher response to this type of statement involves a defensive stance that blames the student for not completing the assignment or even for being rude. However, it is important to recognize that urban students of color are often the victim of a process of schooling that positions them in ways that makes them feel like they are not welcome in school. This forces them to have certain reactions to schooling that can be perceived as inappropriate, and that spark knee-jerk reactions to teachers, who in turn enact knee jerk responses to students because they are unaware of the larger dynamics at play in the classroom.

The chief concept that needs to be grasped by educators, and that will be made throughout this text, is that what is being taught in science classrooms will be perceived by urban students as not significant if the subject delivery methods remain the same. For educators and researchers who choose to work in urban settings with students who are immersed in hip-hop, it must be clear that disinterest, lack of participation, or poor performance is not the result of an intellectual deficiency, or an inability to grasp the content. It is rooted in an inability of educators to teach a new way.

For educators, there must be a shift in the way that we traditionally look at students of color in urban classrooms. There must also be an effort to understand why and how these students' reactions to school and schooling are so visceral, rather than using these reactions as examples of how disinterested they are in school. The teacher must understand that the hip-hop belief system that students ascribe to includes a positioning of oneself as superior to situations at hand in order to both mask one's vulnerability and affirm one's power in situations where one is challenged. This belief system includes a superiority to all that is not explicitly defined as a part of hip-hop culture. Understanding these facts sheds light on the relationship of participants in hip-hop to the science classroom, and highlight the fact that school and science are perceived by youth as trivial in comparison to the complex understandings required to survive in the world and be a part of the highly complex and nuanced culture that is hip-hop.

The perception that school is trivial goes hand in hand with the above-stated hip-hop belief that one is superior to any situation at hand. This superiority complex is evident in the often-haughty dispositions of hip-hop artists in interviews and music videos. It is also seen in the expression of these characteristics by urban youth both within, and outside of, the science classroom. This piece of hip-hop culture (expressing superiority in the face of adversity), is a major component of the ontology of marginalized people of color in the United States. I argue that its roots can be traced to slavery and the moral, stylistic and intellectual superiority expressed by Black slaves in instances where they gathered together to critique their masters cruelty, dress, and mannerisms (Hartman, 1997). I also argue that these historical under-pinnings are the seedbed from which the expressions of a superiority complex in participants in hip-hop take root.

In my work in urban schools, and in my study of the academic work produced on urban education, I find that the issues surrounding this superiority are either understudied or not recognized for what they are. The lack of consideration of the ways of sense making of the hip-hop generation has caused the teaching and learning of urban youth of color to be, and continue to remain inevitably fractured. This is particularly the case in science classrooms because urban youth who are a part of hip-hop are framed as, and then taught as if they are, disinterested in school science. In actuality, their expression of dissatisfaction with the ineffective instruction of the discipline is a marker of interest. The need to actively communicate, present information in colorful and creative ways, or challenge established norms in order to create more complex understandings, that are key components of the hip-hop culture are currently not welcome in urban science classrooms. This is the case in spite of the fact that these above stated "hip-hop attributes" are those that are also beneficial to the advancement of science. For example, the emergence of Einstein's conceptions over pre-established and scientifically accepted Newtonian science is a classic examples of the dominance of thought and creativity over remaining comfortable with conclusions drawn purely from established norms. In the same vein, hip-hop based pedagogy is an advancement over established approaches to teaching science.

In the instruction of science, particularly in urban settings where a majority of students express the extreme thoughtfulness and creativity that comes with being a part of hip-hop, the nature of instruction revolves around the cramming of facts, the omission of the contexts surrounding advances in science, and limited opportunities to utilize one's creativity to make sense of science. Within urban science classrooms, the inability of teachers to understand and accurately reflect the fact that science welcomes the characteristics that participants in hip-hop exhibit outside of the classroom, leads to the continual growth of urban students' negative feelings towards teachers and the positivistic nature of science instruction.

While the pervasiveness of positivism in science has been considered to have waned with the advent of science and technology studies that questions the boundary between science and politics (Jasanoff, 1990), what Fuller (2003) describes as the epistemic status that science enjoys, as well as the problems science has caused and solved in modern society, are generally not considered in urban school science. This, I argue, is a significant factor in hip-hop youths' disenchantment with science, and a cause for both the historical marginalization of hip-hop youth from school, and hip-hop's view of self as beyond school because it does not relate to the brand of science or mathematics that has historically been a part of the urban experience.

Therefore, in a consideration of hip-hop youths' disenchantment with school science, I also consider the historical marginalization of people of color from science. As we progress, I will work towards a reconnecting of the role of this history to what we find in contemporary urban science education. I also work towards fully interrogating contemporary studies of hip-hop as they relate to the urban science classroom. Then, I offer a set of suggestions for the effective instruction of hip-hop youth. I take the step of exploring a historical link because it assists those who are interested in the relationship of science to urban youth experiences to move beyond negative preconceptions of hip-hop and urban youth and consider that the hip-hop generation is an evolved version of the urban poor that Bowles and Gintes (1976) describe as the inhabitors of urban settings in the United States. The overt and purposeful discounting of school that is expressed by hip-hop youth is an outgrowth of silenced responses of the historically oppressed to being excluded from full participation in society. Understanding this fact and its impact on contemporary teaching and learning allows us to see that what we label today as an anti-school hip-hop persona is an expression of a sentiment that pre-dates hip-hop's musical origin in the late 1970s.

One of the most significant connections of hip-hop to its ancestry is in the roots of hip-hop's superiority complex to that of the slave in the mid to late 1880s. I highlight this connection because, as Hayek (1952) mentions, "it is important to observe that in all this, the various types of individual beliefs or attitudes are not themselves the object of our explanation, but merely the elements from which we build up the structure of possible relationships between individuals" (p. 68). In other words, through the exploration of the relationships between the slave and the hip-hop student, our understandings of those within the hip-hop generation are more elaborately developed.

ON SUPERIORITY

For students in urban science classrooms, who are for the most part, largely influenced by, or immersed in hip-hop, they inherit much of the interplay between the overseer and the slave in their experiences within spaces like the urban classroom where they are not given the opportunity to express their hip-hopness. In my work within urban science classrooms, I find that the connections between slavery and the classroom are expressed daily in instances where the student and the teacher's relationship mirrors that of power wielders and the powerless. Since the prototypical urban science classroom is governed by the teacher in a rule by force ideology which focuses on classroom management as the main objective, "doing science work" is presented to students as a necessarily labor intensive set of processes that must be removed from a passion for, or desire to, connect to science. The expected reaction to this relationship between the power wielder and the powerless may be expected to be that the powerless deal with their positioning by internalizing a belief that they are inferior to the power wielders. However, with Black slaves, as with hip-hop youth, the reaction to being positioned as the powerless is a strong sense of self that results in the feeling that they are above the menial tasks presented to them by the master, or in the case of the urban science classroom, the teacher.

If we focus here on the Black slave, the belief in one's superiority is understandable when one looks at the larger circumstances that surrounded slavery. In essence, the need for a self-affirmation in the face of daily debasement can be seen as a necessary coping mechanism. Webber (1978) discusses the slave's belief in "their own stylistic superiority" as expressed in the aversion shown by the quarter community (slave community) for White church services that they found disengaging and lacking in any pleasure. The expression of this superiority was a sentiment that was often expressed in song with lines like, "White folks go to chu'ch, An' he never crack a smile; An' nigger go to chu'ch, an you hear' im' laugh a mile" (Scarborough, 1925, p.168). This lyric displays the nature of the White church sermon, which consisted of the preacher at the pulpit delivering a sermon, or teaching about the word, where the level of engagement is low and full participation is muted. It also describes the Black church, where engagement is high and smiles, laughter, and active engagement are a part of the preaching or teaching.

I argue that the White church service referred to in the slave song is representative of a style of instruction that functions to alienate people whose daily experiences and means of making meaning are multi-modal, and arguably more complex than the simplistic ways of knowing that are required for just sitting and listening. A slave era White church approach to instruction that simply requires sitting and listening cannot connect the hip-hop student to a discipline like science - that requires not just listening, but doing. This is even more the case when the students' hip-hopness dictates that to live is to question.

The result of extracting the students' natural affinity for questioning, and eliminating opportunities for embarking on quests for one's own answers, inevitably breeds a disinterest in science. The result is scenarios where students talk about the teacher and the subject being taught disparagingly while affirming their own intelligence or superiority to what is being taught through by their words and actions. This is seen in conversations that students have in the classroom, their behavior in the classroom, and even hip-hop lyrics like "... while I sleep through class, My teacher can't stand that I always pass, [but I am] Sharp wit da flow like darts wit da flow" (Roscoe, 2003).

For the rapper quoted above, the instruction in class becomes so disengaging that he falls asleep. Concurrently, it describes the student's affirmation of his own intelligence as he describes his sharpness with his rap flow. This lyric is representative of the hip-hop students' belief in their superiority to school, and is the contemporary iteration of the slaves' response to the confining structures that exist in the spaces they are forced to inhabit.

For slaves, the results of dealing with limiting structures in their everyday experiences was the rise of a constant effort to outwit Whites and affirm their superiority over the overseer or master. They met these goals by engaging in practices that were subversive to the master's goals and by making the master the "target of slave jokes and plots" (Webber, 1978). For the hip-hop youth, the master's position as the target of jokes is transferred to the teacher. In my work within urban science classrooms, I have witnessed students purposefully choose not to engage with the subject matter being taught in order to upset or anger the teacher. Under the mask of this show of defiance is a search to find one's superiority to the teacher. The long-term effects of the students' search for the most appropriate response to the constraining structures of the classroom results in the identification of the behaviors that are most frustrating to the teacher or the school, and the purposeful enactment of these behaviors until they are seen as characteristics. These characteristics are then tied to the nature of being hip-hop and not seen as responses to the slavery like nature of instruction within the urban school.

Another misunderstood connection of hip-hop to its slave ancestry is the role of music as one of the chief avenues through which frustration with negative experiences is expressed. Courtlander (1992) describes the fact that slaves would utilize song and rhyme with distinct meter and rhythm (similar to that found in hip-hop) as a means to express their frustration with toiling the fields or a means of generating solidarity when they gathered together. The role of music in the lives of Black slaves mirrors the role that hip-hop music plays with urban youth. The use of the slave song as an avenue for voice can be seen as an example of how rap (one of the chief attributes of hip-hop) has become an avenue for voice for oppressed Black and Latino/a youth. Hip-hop stands as a cultural understanding that has roots in slavery. Once this link is thoroughly investigated, it provides a lens through which educators can look at urban youth that is different from those that are traditionally used. This new vantage point, allows the educator to look at urban youth in ways that go beyond their classroom behaviors, and forces a focus on hip-hop through its historically rich tradition; steeped in the experiences of those who have been and are oppressed. When this new focus on hip-hop and youth in the classroom occurs, what is labeled as poor behavior in school is seen as a search for opportunities to affirm intelligence, and hip-hop becomes the means through which feelings of superiority over the mundane and confining structures of the urban classroom are expressed.

THE TOOLS FOR LIGHTING THE PATH: A THEORETICAL FRAMEWORK
FOR LOOKING AT HIP-HOP AND SCHOOLS

With an understanding of the deep roots of hip-hop having been established, the next step is to provide deeper insight into its relationship to the urban science classroom and move towards teaching a new way. In order to do so, an explicit focus on the theoretical framework that guides the chapters in this book is necessary. Here, I lay out the themes from cultural sociology that speak to the topics that will emerge throughout this work. I present them as pieces of a theoretical framework that provide a deep understanding of hip-hop, science, and education and the ways that they indelibly affect each other and impact the instruction of youth in urban science classrooms.

On Cultural Sociology and the Use of Structure

Cultural sociology is a field of study that functions to "bring the unconscious cultural structures that regulate society into the light of the mind" (Alexander, 2005 p. 3). In other words, it functions to question unquestioned social structures that impact the ways that we act and brings the results of this questioning to the forefront of our discussions. This approach can be seen as a means to explain the whys and hows of our daily interactions and the social phenomena that shape them. Cultural sociology provides a framework for seeing how hip-hop has evolved into a democratic space for those who have been denied the opportunity to be active participants in a democratic society at large, and within schools.

I have already mentioned, and will consistently refer to structure. In many cases, I will refer to the relationship between structure and agency and the fact that the agency or power to act for an individual or group is related to the structures in place within a social setting. For example, for hip-hop students in the classroom, both their agency and the way that this agency is enacted is dependent upon both animate and inanimate structures like the teacher and the materials in the class. Therefore, structures stand as objects or phenomena within social life that provide a frame for another aspect of social existence (Sewell, 1992). The frame that structures provide can then be viewed as parameters that a person or group must function under or within in order to exist. For example, the fact that science is taught in an urban science classroom by limiting hands on demonstrations (in comparison with classes in non-urban schools who are more socioeconomically advantaged), or not supporting inquiry creates a scenario where the agency of students in the classroom to engage in hands on activities that would provide more than superficial insight or interest into science is limited. When a student is not free to explore scientific concepts using hands on or inquiry based tools, the structure created by the teacher, or the nature of the urban classroom, is invariably linked to the limited agency of students in the classroom to be fully connected to science.

Structure and Agency

Sewell (1992) makes it clear that structures shape practices, but it is also people's practices that constitute (and reproduce) structures. This reciprocal relationship between structure and agency stands as a way to make sense of the constant affirmation and reaffirmation of structures that impact human practices and the evolution of practices into patterns of behavior that become seen as characteristics. This is the case because once a structure is in place that leads to the enactment of a set of practices; the practices become a way through which the structure is reaffirmed. This interplay between structure and agency is ultimately rooted in culture. For example, the oppressive structures within urban settings that prevented poor urban Black and Latino/a youth from having the monetary and symbolic resources to be involved in the party scene in the late 1970s created certain constraints on the extent to which they could be a part of the larger social scene. These constraining structures pushed them to be able to enact agency in very limited ways that were outside of the larger party scene. This resulted in their creation of an alternate social scene. They began throwing parties in the parks in their neighborhoods, and before long, hip-hop was born. In the creation of hip-hop, the larger structures that were put in place affected urban youth agency. Ultimately, this agency became enacted in a way that led to the advent of hip-hop. Hip-hop stood as a way to enact agency within the parameters set by the established culture and over time, evolved into a distinct culture. With all this being said, it is important to also recognize that "societies are based on practices that derive from many distinct cultures, which exist at different levels, operate in different modalities, and are themselves based on varying types and quantities of resources" (Sewell, 1992, p. 16).

On Culture

The use of the word cultures by Sewell in the above quote makes it a key piece of the theoretical framework developed for making meaning of hip-hop and identifying characteristics that one could classify as hip-hopness. This focus on culture lays the groundwork for a deeper understanding of what it means to be part of the hip-hop generation within a school with a culture that is other than hip-hop. A discussion of culture also assists in the sense making of urban school science and the fact that is has its own distinct culture. The view of culture I hold begins with the fundamental understanding that culture is composed of schema and practices. This view of culture is an extraction of a definition from Sewell's discussion on the relationship between structure and agency as he discusses the role of practices and the multi-modality of structure. However, it is more deeply rooted in a Bourdieusian frame-work and can be seen as a contemporary explication of the fact that the knowledge imposed on students in schools is founded on the culture of the dominant class, which determines what is taught in schools (Bourdieu & Passeron, 1977). Class and culture are therefore related and the societal value placed on certain schema and practices determines whether they are of a certain societally valued or devalued class.

Extending the example of hip-hop and its formation as a result of structures that inhibited the connection of urban youth to the social scene, I argue that the creation of hip-hop culture from the structures that sought to set the parameters for the enactment of agency for urban youth of color, relegated hip-hop to a low class culture or lower class structure than the culture that it grew in response to. In weaving the theoretical pieces from the previous two paragraphs into this one, I argue that the structures that are in place within a social field are directly related to, or implemented by, the larger culture in place. There are cultures that grow because they are considered the popular or higher class culture and then there are those that grow because they are responses to those mentioned above. Certain cultures serve the interest of the dominant class and the reciprocal relationship between structure and agency functions to reaffirm these structures and reproduce power dynamics. In the case of school science, particularly in urban schools, the teacher functions as the power wielder and the representative of not only the power structure of the school, but that of "Western" science. Therefore, students who are a part of a culture that developed in response to the larger dominant culture are positioned in ways that cause their culture to be perpetually devalued by school unless there is a fracture in the continuum between structure and agency. In other words, if a culture is birthed out of a response to an existent one, it quite possibly is based on tenets that are critiques of the established culture. Therefore, it will be positioned as less than the dominant culture as long as the power of that larger culture is maintained. In many ways, hip-hop stands as a response to an established culture. However, over time, it has evolved to interrupt the continuum between structure and agency that sustains the existent culture and has become its own distinct established culture.

The relationship between structure and agency, and the role of culture in this relationship is also seen in science education. In this field of study, there is a focus on the nature of science, inquiry, and other more constructivist approaches to instruction that breed certain schema and practices that give the discipline a certain culture. However, in the relationship between science education and urban science education (which itself has its own distinct culture), the structures in place within urban science education extract much of the practices that are identified by science education as necessary for teaching science. In place of constructivist approaches to instruction there is a hyper focus on issues like classroom management. In a sense, approaches to instruction that are valuable for all students are removed from urban science education. Hence, Bourdieu's (1984) discussion of the inclination of dominant culture/class to remove practical use or material necessity from education gets played out within urban science classrooms. This issue is problematic for students who are a part of a culture like hip-hop, which is based on hands on teaching and learning and the enactment of practical responses to issues that affect one's community.

Focusing on Social Fields and Capital

In an extension of Bourdieu's work, I utilize his (1983) notion of the social field and his examination of capital to analyze our topic of discussion further. I view hip-hop, schools, and science as separate social fields in which certain types of

17

culture are simultaneously produced, reproduced, and transformed, and certain capital is held and or exchanged. There are certain understandings in hip-hop, schools, and science that are distinct to each, and under which participants in each of the fields are consistently operating. For example, the ways that students communicate in a hip-hop field where they are writing a rap together varies significantly from the ways that teachers expect the students to communicate with each other in a classroom. While students may collaborate to create a rap song, and suggest ways to improve each rap verse, the classroom teacher may expect each student to be individually responsible for providing answers to questions she asks. Each social world, whether affiliated with hip-hop, schools, or science, is made up of what Bourdieu refers to as an "accumulated history" based for a large part on the experiences of participants in the culture (Bourdieu, 1983). This view validates the perspective that hip-hop as a culture that is historically rooted in slavery and gets enacted within certain social fields, and school and science as separate entities each with its own distinct history gets enacted in other fields like classrooms or the school. Bourdieu describes these fields as systems within which participants interact and exchange different forms of capital (Bourdieu, 1990). By capital here, I refer primarily to social capital and the fact that "social capital is defined by its function. It is not a single entity, but a variety of different entities... and they facilitate certain actions of actors" (Coleman, 1998, p. 103).

Viewing the environments where culture is produced as fields is helpful for assisting the reader in looking at the dynamics at play among people of a particular culture in different spaces. For example, when participants in hip-hop are rapping to each other on a street corner, they are in a social field expressing their cultural and social capital. Within social fields that are outside of the classroom, they will inevitably express a part of this culture, and may either be supported or hindered from doing so depending on the structure within the field they are in. When students rap within a social network of their peers in the field of the rap cypher, there is a situation where there is a type of capital that is unique to the field that is supported by the structures within it. Conversely, in a classroom, where the teacher is teaching a lesson to students who share a similar cultural background with the teacher, they are interacting with each other in a field where they have the opportunity to exchange similar types of capital. The teacher and the objects in the classroom are structures, and these structures facilitate the types of actions or behaviors that students enact.

The Structures of the School

By looking at hip-hop and urban schools as separate fields, each with different structures that sometimes have the same actors or participants, it becomes easy to see the ways in which actors from both of these fields interact when they come in contact with each other in the classroom. By looking at the classroom as a social field where two types of people with different forms of capital come together, one is able to look at the dynamics at play when hip-hop culture becomes expressed in the classroom and understand the ways that this clash of cultures affects teaching and learning. In a school, the actors in the larger social field are teachers, school administrators and students. In the larger field of hip-hop, the actors in the field are graffiti artists, rap artists, dancers, deejays and those who appreciate their genre. When participants in hip-hop come into schools, and particularly when they enter into the science classroom, the nature of the new field, or the structures of the field (the classroom) are often different from those in the fields they inhabit outside of the classroom. This in turn, affects the students' agency.

There is a separation between the culture in hip-hop fields and those of school fields that requires participants in hip-hop to maneuver through the structures of schools in order to find ways to enact their agency in ways that allow them to be successful in classrooms. To communicate in the classroom, a participant in hip-hop has to understand the ways to appropriately communicate in this field and ensure that there is no indication of her hip-hop identity in this communication. This separation of cultures is primarily a function of the low value assigned to hip-hop culture in schools and the subsequent implementation of structures within schools that are intended to limit the agency of participants in hip-hop. Oftentimes, the structures that limit the student's agency are teachers that adhere to a too-strict curriculum limited to too-few topics that are often not presented in new ways that incite student interest. These structures also include school regulations that consequently limit access to materials that would allow students to engage in science. The limiting structure of the hyper-strict curriculum draws invisible lines which confine each group of actors in the classroom (students, teachers, administrators) into pockets that cause them to either not consider the social capital of others as valuable or to explicitly work to de-legitimize the culture of others in the schooling process. An example of how these divides become enacted is often evident in the urban schools where I conduct research.

In these fields, teachers follow a pre-established curriculum and do not deviate from the existent state mandated plan. Furthermore, they focus on referencing learning standards and performance indicators rather than examples of science and teaching referent points from students' lifeworlds. Teacher practice is too often completely aligned to an established plan that does not reflect the diversity of the students being forced to adhere to these standards, and does not function to generate student interest. In one classroom, an experienced chemist who had been involved in numerous research projects around the world prior to becoming a science teacher found that there was such a limit on his capital that he could not teach chemistry in a way that reflected his experiences of doing extensive research in the discipline. The strict limits on what to teach and how to teach negated the experience he had gained as a chemist and the potential for engaging students in new ways. In other words, the possible ways to utilize his expertise to involve students in the subject were severely limited by the structures of the science curriculum. In one particular instance, a teacher responded to a student's request to spend some extra time on a science topic she was interested in by saying "We have no time to improvise here, I don't make this up. This (what I teach) is from the state and we have limited time for nomenclature."

Within this structure, the teacher who is a chemist is devalued in order to become a teacher. Therefore, the student who is immersed in hip-hop is forced into the even more lowly position of the victim of an established approach to education implemented by a possibly effective educator that is rendered powerless because of an approach to instruction he is forced to adopt.

As I sit and write this, more than four decades after the lyric that asked teachers to teach a new way made its way to the general public, and less than two decades after I first stumbled upon the record that introduced me to this question, it appears as though not much has changed. The issue for connecting students to the subject matter is more pressing than it has ever been. Therefore, I continue in this work holding tightly to my strong allegiances to students and teachers in urban science classrooms. I write not only from my stance as an academic but also from my stance as a participant in hip-hop. I draw upon my experiences as teacher and researcher and write from my stance as a man of color, having completed a vast majority of my education in urban public institutions. Through this position I hold an intimate, reflexive, phenomenological, and experiential view of what learning and teaching science in urban settings entails. I am a product of the social and temporal structures that shape the contexts wherein I am embedded and set the parameters for how I enact my agency. They guide my path into this work. I am a scientist, I am an educator and I am hip-hop.

FROM 1520 SEDGWICK TO THE WORLD: MASKED BUT NOT ERASED

It is a windy fall evening in the Bronx and I stand at the entrance to Cedar Park absorbing all the science that oozes out of every inch of space before me. I see kinematics in the cars driving by, sound waves from a nearby radio, and, genetics lessons in the varied complexions of the people walking past. I pull a note pad from my pocket and try to capture the excitement I feel from experiencing this living science lesson. This is what I am after. I want to make the physical and life science classes I teach come to life for my middle school students; students who have traditionally been both turned away and turned off by science. To forge a new connection I need to understand the historical injustices that continue to wield influence over this neighbourhood as well as the reality of day-to-day life near Cedar Park.

The wind that whistles in my ear serves a perfect backdrop to the dance of the yellow and orange leaves that cascade to the floor of the park. This song and dance echoes the history of this park and the apartment building that both physically and symbolically towers over the neighborhood. Hip-hop was born at 1520 Sedgwick Avenue, just down the street from Cedar Park. Song and dance are a part of the history of this park but the park's significance goes much deeper than song and dance. The park is part of the setting to the creation of hip-hop, is symbolic of hip-hop in its purest form, and is a testament to the ingenuity of people of color who have often been marginalized from attainment in school and in science in particular. Without the socioeconomic status to be considered full participants in society, oppressed Black and Brown youth struggled to have their voices heard - particularly within schools. Cedar Park and 1520 Sedgwick Avenue came to represent a beacon of hope in the Bronx, in the 1970s. There was something about the song and dance in those locations that grew into an escape from a present reality, and then into a shared understanding that developed into a distinct culture. The physical spaces (Cedar Park and 1520 Sedgwick Avenue) became places where urban Black and Brown youth were able to move beyond the tyranny of their schools and society in general, albeit temporarily, and escape into a world where they were accepted. Such spaces became a refuge where participants in hip-hop saw themselves as whole and excellent. It is in these spaces that I search for ways to connect students who are a part of the hip-hop culture to science.

At certain points in the United States' history, it too has stood as a refuge. For populations across the globe it has been perceived to stand at the forefront of providing social, economic and educational opportunity when the structures in other places inhibited it. For many people, it still stands as a beacon of hope as they fight insurmountable obstacles to fully participate in the socioeconomic and socio-political worlds both within and beyond their places of origin. Across the world, people have deeply desired to be part of this progressive society where the refrain of "excellence for all" seems not only possible, but also tangible. The words "liberty and justice for all" seem to be not just empty words from the nation's pledge of allegiance, but a believable refrain that calls forth all the hope and determination that the depths of an oppressed soul can carry. Kool Herc, considered by many to be the originator of hip-hop, came from a family that saw the United States as a refuge. He was born in Kingston, Jamaica and migrated to the United States with his family in hopes for a brighter future. In a sense, his life journey, and that of hip-hop, is the story of millions of people in the United States.

For many who are outside of the country, delusions of equity and excellence within the United States are plastered across their imaginations. Thoughts about what the country can provide combine with expectations of scientific, social, and educational excellence and merge with visions of streets of gold to take root in many imaginations. One high school student that I interviewed, whose parent emigrated from Ghana, West Africa mentioned that he always thought that the United States was a place where "you would press a button, and anything you wanted would come to you. If you wanted, food, a car, clothes, or money you could just press a button and it would come."

The roots of the perceived excellence of the United States, can be tied to the nation's founding fathers, who themselves, escaped the tyranny of their places of origin to begin a new nation. These founding fathers are positioned in United States history as a group of men who were on a quest for a new beginning and ended up blazing a new trail. However, for the founders of this country, the fight for freedom encompassed not only a quest for democracy, but also a commitment to innovation, new thinking, and new ideas. The birth of the nation was not only an exercise in starting anew and blazing a new trail, but was an active effort to recreate norms as agreed upon by the citizens of the nation. In a sense, it is the story of hip-hop. Creating something innovative that speaks to the uniqueness of individuals who previously have been collectively ostracized is both American and hip-hop.

Benjamin Franklin, who is considered a forefather of the United States, and who signed the Declaration of Independence, was not only a proponent of democracy, but also a scientist and inventor. His story is often framed as the story of the United States - in the sense that for Franklin, both political and democratic sensibilities merged with scientific ability to make the man. Kool Herc expressed this same merging of abilities as he utilized his knowledge of music, ability to transfer cultural understandings from Jamaica to the Bronx, and democratic sensibility (in the opening of hip-hop to all who were oppressed by life in the city and beyond.) in creating hip-hop. In fact, the only pre-requisite to becoming a part of hip-hop is an expression of genuineness in one's relationship to, and expression of, the culture. This single pre-requisite allows for the constant re-evolution of hip-hop that is only matched by the constantly changing demographics of the United States.

Maintaining a false excellence

In the years after the age of Benjamin Franklin, the doors of the United States have been open to those who have had the ability to embody a spirit of political and scientific ingenuity. The number of scientists from around the world who have crossed their shores to become a part of the United States up to the late 1950's are almost innumerable. The United States welcomed all those who embodied a spirit of ingenuity that could be translated into excellence in academic arenas. The culture of excellence that was generated in this era bled into the nation's fabric and even today, the U.S. Department of Education carries an ethos of "Promoting Educational Excellence for All Americans" (USDOE, 2009). This focus on excellence for all is part and parcel of a desire to affirm the nation's guiding ethos of being a nation of immigrants and position it as ahead of its counterparts.

In an attempt to maintain the picture of perfection that the United States held across the globe, any indication that excellence was not possible or feasible for the nation was responded to by a conscious move by the powers that be to ensure that the erasure of such a thought was not only seen, but also felt. For example, the Soviet launching of a satellite into orbit before the United States in 1957 was a sign of a possible fallibility or fall from excellence for the nation. True to form, the response was a vigorous move to erase any thought that the nation was sub-par in comparison to anywhere else in the world (US Information Agency,1959). There was an immediate increase in funding for science education and a drastic change in curriculum so that it would develop more students who would become scientists. Students in public institutions were steered towards science and consequently, interest in science increased. In fact, it has been argued that the last concentrated national initiative to improve math and science education was in the 1960s, in response to Sputnik (Carey, 2001). Before long, American astronauts were the first to set foot on the Moon and re-established the perception of the United States' excellence in the scientific arena. On July 20, 1969, the day that American astronauts set foot on the moon, there was a perceived erasure of the Soviet accomplishment by a greater United States' one. Through this monumental achievement, there seemed to be a reinstatement of the belief that the nation was once again dominant and as close to perfect as ever possible (Rudolph, 2002). However, the problem with an attempt to erase other entities' accomplishments in an effort to bring complete attention to ones' own is that ignoring or masking the other is not an erasure. The past accomplishment still exists and a temporary eclipse does not mean that the light beneath never existed and won't shine again. It is at this point (erasure of an entity other than the nation) that the variance between the hip-hop story and the story of the United States comes to light.

The process of masking as a way to erase another entity has always been apparent in the United States. It is evident in the way that the public attempts to erase the accomplishments, or even the presence, of those among its people that are perceived as being far from the prevailing notion of excellence. It is the nation-wide ignoring of the Native Americans in the United States, the clamour to move beyond slavery and its perpetual implications on the lives of people of color, and the leaving behind of millions of students of lower socioeconomic backgrounds in urban schools as a result of the No Child Left Behind Act. However, despite these efforts to erase certain populations, the reality is that erasure is quite different from masking, and that masking, covering, or ignoring can never erase. In the case of people of color within the United States, attempts to erase their plight by ignoring the after effects of slavery and institutionalized racism has resulted in the creation of hip-hop culture; which has gathered populations of every race and creed in support of the plight of the marginalized. While the marginalized may be temporarily masked, they are never erased.

Despite the great United States' accomplishment of July 20th 1969, the Soviet launch of Sputnik still existed. It was a monumental event and an enduring scientific achievement. Although there was a greater United States' achievement that came after the Soviet launch, their initial accomplishment fuelled the Soviet Union's passion to develop its people to achieve in the sciences. As the United States attempted to erase events, a more realistic perspective suggests it only plastered, and still plasters wallpaper on cracks in their wall of excellence. It masked the Soviet accomplishment and simultaneously attempted to mask the existence of people within the nation who were perceived as far from excellent. Those who were to be erased within the nation were believed to be a deficiency or a presence that taints the nation's perfection. Despite the fact that these people could never be either masked or erased per se, they are still targeted as hindrances to the excellence of the nation.

The demographically large yet neglected sectors of the population who by historical circumstances in the United States have been economically impoverished, educationally neglected, and faced the brunt of racial and social class prejudice collectively define themselves as hip-hop. They are both the victims of slavery and their ancestors, for the ancestors and direct victims bear the same emotional and psychological scars. They are the primarily Black and Latino/a youth in the inner cities and beyond who are not considered to be worthy of attaining the American dream, and are also the multitudes of hyphenated-Americans from various ethnic and racial backgrounds who have been localized to schools that have failed to uniformly provide all people with a high quality education. As we tout excellence within urban public institutions in the United States, and ignore the needs of an ever-growing population whose needs are not addressed within schools, we continue a legacy of attempted erasure. We continue to mask because we cannot erase.

The unmasking

When one looks back at the United States and its response to the Sputnik launch, it becomes clear that there was an effort to create a larger U.S accomplishment, and also an intense focus on science education. In the focus on science education, youth of color were excluded from programs that led students to science and were deemed as unable to participate in the sciences. Minority youth were locked into sub-standard schools and were prohibited from full participation in the sciences because of societal perceptions of their intellectual capabilities. As we look forward to the future of the United States, we see that those who have been labelled as minorities, and who have been excluded from science, are "expected to become the majority in 2042. By 2050, the nation is projected to be 54 percent minority. In fact, "by 2023, minorities will comprise more than half of all children" (U.S. Census, 2008).

At this juncture, it is important to recognize that those who have been labelled as intellectually inferior because they were a minority are now a majority. In order to make sense of the attempted erasure of these populations, and concurrently maintain the United States' excellence, we must concurrently look backwards and forwards. Looking towards the past, we must ask whether all students were equally pushed to do well in science after the push for science education reform after the Sputnik launch. Were all their interests piqued? Was there only a focus on who was perceived to be important and able to make a difference? Looking towards the future, we must ask, what are the affects of the attempted erasure of particular populations on the future scientific excellence of the nation? Any thorough interrogation of these questions reveals that many were intentionally erased from full participation in science. The discipline was viewed as a proper endeavor for only a selected few who were perceived as having the intellectual capability to do well. Others were treated as though they did not exist. Their existence as future scientists seemed to have been erased.

Addressing the needs of people of color in the United States is absolutely necessary, and this is the pressing challenge that we currently have in urban science education. With this focus, the future does not have to be as bleak and the past can be not just painful memories, but a learning tool. The narrative of exclusion and deficiency that we appear predestined to inherit may very well be the avenue through which both science education and the urban education community reach a perspective of hope and realization.

While the larger social and economic inequities commonly suffered by urban youth have implications beyond the field of education, the key issue for the purposes of this body of work is to address these inequities through a focus on connecting urban youth to science and reframing urban science education to more directly meet their needs.

Educators who believe in providing students of all racial, ethnic and socio-cultural backgrounds equal access to science have already begun to look at the inequities in science education as a social justice issue (Tate, 2001). For these researchers, urban settings have proven to be sites where much needed change in access and exposure to science can begin. Students within present urban science classrooms call for this change through their behavior in classrooms, and the messages in hip-hop. They no longer want to be tied down by misconceptions of their intellectual ability and want to be unmasked and seen for their potential to do well in science classrooms. While their call for change is important to recognize, it cannot be achieved without the realization that the academic/educational challenges that have plagued these communities are compounded with years of disregard, invalidation, and the general positioning of the urban student as other than the "normal" student. The normal student is perceived as interested in school, seen as having the ability to succeed, and most importantly, supported to succeed in science. Those who are perceived as other than this normal student are alienated from full participation in school and consequently are removed from success in science. The collateral effects of being alienated from the norm (not being viewed or treated as the normal student) in conjunction with the absence of material resources for engaging in a discipline like science, have formed huge gaps between the culture of school and that of many urban students. These issues are compounded by the fact that the science curriculum within urban schools has itself become a norm that is far removed from the culture of the hip-hop generation.

As facts about the various issues that work towards keeping participants in hip-hop from science get revealed, and as we peel the layers of the complexities that are the walls of our existence, issues such as the alliances that urban students have formed to each other under the banner of hip-hop, their angst for schools, and choices to not engage in school science become more understood and justified. Through hip-hop, an entire generation has laid out the tools through which urban youth can become unmasked, connected to science, and become a part of the American quest for excellence.

As we examine the complex dynamics that inhibit achievement in science for students of hip-hop in urban classrooms, I investigate both the present experiences and histories of this population and their relationship to education and hip-hop. I grasp the need to engage in research that aims to be authentic and representative with as little personal idiosyncratic bias as possible, while also acknowledging the importance of my obligation to reveal, provide voice to, and expose the realities for students in these settings through my experience. To meet this goal, I close this chapter much as I did the last, by standing upon my experiences in urban schools and once again calling forth my experiences as student, teacher, administrator, and researcher.

I present my subjectivity not as a bias, but as a means to provide further insight into the approaches to teaching and research that are necessary for unmasking urban youth in schools. As a teacher and researcher, I must wear my past experiences within urban settings and schools on my sleeve and make no apologies for my position. I must hold on to who I am, and concurrently utilize the authenticity criteria outlined by Guba and Lincoln (1989) to ensure that my research, and the scholarship that is produced from it, is tactical, authentic, ontological, and catalytic for all students and research participants. I must work to ensure that what I do rings true for those I work to bring to school, and makes a genuine difference in their lives. The position I have carved out as a teacher, urban science educator, and researcher must guide my interrogation of the contexts within urban science classrooms, and should be a major component of what is required to conduct research and teach in urban science classrooms. This is why I look to teach participants in hip-hop, by immersing myself in contexts like Cedar Park. I argue that this is the true means through which teaching a new way, unmasking the potential of the hip-hop generation, and finally connecting urban youth to school and science can begin.

CHAPTER 4

WE ARE HIP-HOP AND SCHOOL IS NOT

SITUATING HIP-HOP, RAP AND URBAN SCIENCE EDUCATION

On a Wednesday afternoon, three weeks into a new school year, I stood in the back of a chemistry classroom in the Bronx and watched a sea of half asleep black and brown faces painted with confusion, frustration, and indifference as a teacher practically did pirouettes in a dance of figures, chemicals and atoms trying to get the students' attention to no avail. A few minutes after I became settled in the back of the class, the sound of a rap song drifted into the room from a passing car. Almost immediately, most of the students sat up and almost simultaneously began nodding their heads to the beat. Students looked up at each other and smiled. Others mouthed the words of the song under their breath. They gave each other knowing glances that were acknowledged with slight head nods from their peers and eye contact that signified that there was something that collectively garnered all of their attention. There was an obvious emotional energy generated by the song that drifted into the classroom that the teacher's lesson did not provide.

As the car slowly drove past, the sound of the song dissipated into muffled bass and a faint drum pattern. The distinctive beat of the song faded into silence and was replaced by the repetitive ticking of the clock in front of the class. The students' smiles faded into blank stares and as the teacher kept talking, and the lesson proceeded, the students slowly returned to their narcoleptic state.

Surreal moments like the one I experienced this day occur often in urban science classrooms and signify a connection between hip-hop and urban science education that has yet to be made, but lies ready to be discovered. These moments are an indication that there exists, complex, and nuanced connections between hip-hop and school. Furthermore, if these connections are properly acknowledged and validated, they lead to the transformation of both arenas (hip-hop and school) for the benefit of science teaching, learning and research in urban settings. Validating the connection between hip-hop and school is an arduous and controversial task because bringing hip-hop culture into schools is viewed as synonymous with bringing urban Black culture and all the negative stereotypes associated with it into formal institutions of learning. However, while hip-hop does have roots in Black culture, it is not exclusive to urban Black youth. This misconception about the Blackness of hip-hop in conjunction with the oftentimes racist perceptions of Black youth serve as a major hindrance to the objective viewing of hip-hop and exploration of its potential to inform urban science education.

Within urban schools, where a vast majority of students are participants in hip-hop culture, having a process where hip-hop is objectively viewed and accurately described is not a consideration. The fundamental reason for the invalidation of this link between hip-hop and school/science is a general lack of recognition of hip-hop as a valued culture or way of being. In addition, there is a misunderstanding about hip-hop culture that causes it to be perceived as counterproductive to producing or becoming a successful student. This lack of recognition of hip-hop within schools combines with a strict adherence to a preferred corporate teaching and learning ideology rampant in urban science education that blinds educators to the transformative qualities inherent in the localized, more communal understandings of urban youth. By this, I mean that the ways to most appropriately teach a specific population in an effective manner requires a focus on the ways that they communicate with each other and the communal nature of their lifeworlds outside of school and in their local surroundings.

The Structure of Hip-hop: Rappers, Deejays, B-boys and Emcees

The ways that participants in hip-hop communicate is most evident within a study of the key strands of hip-hop. These strands are graffiti, Deejaying, Rapping (emceeing) and breakdancing (b-boying). Within each strand, and among the three strands, participants are all of equal value. In fact, the outside participants (onlookers/audience) are just as much a component of the culture as the performer or presenter. Hip-hop therefore serves as a field where a sort of cosmopolitan ideal is achieved. Because the communication among participants in the culture begins from the point where everyone has an opportunity to speak and be valued, every participant is empowered and therefore is supportive of each other. The attributes of a good deejay or hype man are not only admired, but are revered by other communities within the culture. The ability to move a crowd and make an audience move in unison as they hang on every word of a prolific emcee is perceived as the ultimate form of expression by every participant in hip-hop culture. The depth, painstaking accuracy, and fluidity of movement of a graffiti artist or breakdancer (B-boy) are perceived as iconic by both rappers and deejays. The culture, therefore, becomes the ultimate expression of the act of accepting multiple sub-cultures and valuing all participants. Within hip-hop, participants from varying racial and ethnic backgrounds function with a desire to better the culture as they show the unique skills that they have within the particular part of the culture they are most involved in. In a hip-hop event, participants from each part of the culture have a role to play. In fact certain social engagements do not function properly unless rappers, deejays and b-boys are fully engaged. The provision of agency to express capital is integral to the functioning of hip-hop and is one of the reasons why the culture has developed the ability to constantly re-invent itself with new participants.

Another very important attribute of hip-hop, and reason for its incredibly complex communicative aspects, is how the culture fosters and admires the ability to improvise. The ability to freestyle rap (creating raps on the spot), which requires engaging an audience by focusing on what both a performer and audience have in common at a specific space in time, shows the culture's ability to be malleable and embrace all from "a gentle child like rapper to...roughneck MC's" (George, 1999, p. 154). Supernatural, a rapper world renowned for his ability to freestyle, often talks about how improvisation is the key to freestyle and how there are no time restraints or parameters to getting an audience involved in freestye. "When someone throws a word out there, I create a rap about it on the spot to get them involved and communicate with them."

For students who are a part of the hip-hop culture, one of the most significant misunderstandings about their culture is that hip-hop is something that they choose to partake in or have the choice to either participate in or not. I argue that it is the culture of youth in urban settings. Even when students listen to other genres of music, or come from homes where hip-hop music is forbidden, in order to, communicate in an effective manner within certain urban settings, it is necessary to embrace a certain hip-hopness. In fact, it is impossible to successfully interact with one's peers in the urban spaces where minoritized populations dwell without having some type of hip-hop sensibility.

I Choose Hip-hop, I Need Hip-hop

For many people, hip-hop is seen as something that a person becomes involved in because he has an affinity for certain parts of, or is temporarily enamored by artifacts developed from hip-hop like rap or graffiti. While this may be the case in certain communities that are afforded the socioeconomic allowances to engage in an activity such as a hip-hop aerobic class or who occasionally watch a rap video for leisure, those whose lifeworlds surround hip-hop have no choice but to be a part of the culture.

For populations who are not a part of hip-hop culture but who have chosen to engage in hip-hop, the need to be fully immersed in hip-hop is not as necessary. For example, it has become normal to see hip-hop dance classes being offered in the same arenas as ballet classes in affluent communities. In some instances, it is commonplace to see a hip-hop clothing store next to a high-end designer store in a shopping mall. The audience that engages in this commodified brand of hip-hop has an interesting relationship with the culture that involves a superficial acceptance of hip-hop and a concurrent fear of what making it a part of their lifeworlds truly means.

This commercial acceptance and commodification of hip-hop causes many people in communities outside of the locales where hip-hop has traditionally lived to believe that it is one of many identity options for a person to choose. In reality, hip-hop is a lifestyle and in many cases, it is the only thing that gives agency to those in contexts that are far from the mainstream whose true existences have been masked in urban science classrooms. When I refer to hip-hop, or when students in urban communities refer to it, it is not seen as a title or label. Urban youth see themselves as hip-hop. My research indicates that urban youth, who are marginalized from achievement in science, see themselves as not only participants in hip-hop, but as a living embodiment of the culture. In New York City, the birthplace of hip-hop, and the site for much of my work, the phrase "I am Hip-hop" is a slogan that is not only printed across t-shirts and spouted from the lips of students, but is engrained in their identities. As one of the students in a physics class I taught, and where I conducted research, eloquently stated in a research dialogue that will be discussed later in this work, "hip-hop is what makes us, us."

Science and Hip-hop as Culture

The notion, that hip-hop is a culture made up of not only the practices or activities of a population but the shared understandings of a group of people and the way they view the world, aligns auspiciously with the culture of science. The culture of science, which Cordero (2001) refers to as a "scientific picture of the world" is made up of the way that scientists view the world. Likewise, the culture of hip-hop refers to the way that its participants view and make sense of their world.

This relationship between hip-hop and science can be seen in the fact that science, which possesses a certain epistemic value, positions itself as being an international language that is accessible to all. Ridley (2001) discusses the prevalence of what he terms scientism, which is the belief that science has the ability to see itself as able to make sense of everything in the world. Science, which is a distinct way of knowing, is presented to the world as being accessible to everyone who is willing to be a part of it.

Hip-hop, which is a culture whose main artifacts are perceived as related to the arts, correlates to science because "From an Apollonian point of view, both science and art aim for an understanding of the world; both appear to be part of an understanding of the world; both appear to be part of an all-embracing culture of enquiry, a search for all forms of truth" (Ridley, 2001, p. 1). Furthermore, the most fundamental connection of hip-hop to science is that hip-hop is the voice of urban youth and built on passionate response to one's physical and social surroundings. "Scientists are, believe it or not, human, and often motivated by passions that are far from being scientific" (Ridely, p. 65). Essentially, the omission of hip-hop culture from urban schools that are in the communities where hip-hop is created, limits the process of connecting hip-hop to science even though they are phenomena that are already fundamentally connected. This process is counter-intuitive to instructional techniques that rest on connecting students to science through their lifeworlds and experiences. It also relegates teaching to archaic, hyper-structured instruction rather than an inquiry and interest-based approach to delivering subject matter that focuses on the fact that both hip-hop and science are entities that provide a picture of the world from a particular group's perspective.

Structures within schools like school personnel and their belief systems, that do not consider the ways that people view the world, actually interrupt the process of having students whose worldview has been masked from becoming active parts of the schooling process. These structures support reductionist approaches to instruction and viewing the world, that require individuals who are involved in highly communal practices based on oral traditions, community, coteaching and colearning to remove themselves from their norms and adopt an alien approach to teaching and learning. Oliver (2001) clearly outlines the contradictory logic of these types of reductionist processes through her descriptions of colonial authority and its "contradiction between denying the internal life, mind, or soul to the colonized on one hand, and demanding that they internalize colonial values on the other" (p.30). In other words, within the traditional science classroom, a colonization of the hip-hop participant, which can be seen as domination over students' words, thoughts and ideas, and a relegation of their position to other than norm becomes common practice.

In this colonization process, hip-hop participants' ways of being in the world are denied opportunity to become expressed in the classroom and these students are forced to follow the routines of a science classroom that are opposed to their ways of viewing the world. For example, a student who is accustomed to working with peers in solving real life problems in the hip-hop fields outside of the classroom, when forced to work within an urban science classroom that is focused on individual success, will have a challenge connecting to the classroom, and will eventually disconnect from science.

This type of practice clearly outlines the reasons why urban students who are a part of hip-hop are often unsuccessful within schools and science. While the urban science classroom limits hip-hop students' opportunities to express their culture in the classroom, they are forced to embrace the culture of the colonizer and be silent, docile, and passive in order to be successful within school science. This is the case even if their expression of hip-hop includes attributes that support their engagement in science. Attributes of participants in hip-hop, like speaking with one's hands or raising one's voice to get another person's attention, may be looked at as subverting the teacher's control over the classroom rather than an expression of interest. This creates a dilemma where what is considered appropriate behavior for learning science in urban classrooms actually constricts certain students' ability to engage, participate, and experience success in the science classroom.

What's so Great About Hip-Hop?

My goal here is not to describe a false utopia of hip-hop or to label school science as completely alien to certain populations. In fact, there are pockets within both hip-hop and school that serve as counter-examples to the descriptions I have laid out. However, on a grand scale, my research indicates that participants in hip-hop generally view science classrooms as fields that impede their excitement about learning new things or actively participating in an activity. By contrast, they view fields within hip-hop as supporters of these processes. Juxtaposing the descriptions of the school field with the hip-hop field, it becomes evident that the hierarchical nature of interactions amongst actors in urban schools is among the major reasons why students who are participants in hip-hop do not feel comfortable interacting within urban schools.

The improvisational nature of hip-hop combines with its value for communality and is the key to its lasting legacy and longevity. Despite consistent commentary throughout its existence that it is just a musical fad, hip-hop has a stable history that makes allowances for its evolution within the socio-political landscapes and contexts where the culture is lived. There is also a consistent push within hip-hop to find new ways to connect to new audiences. If police brutality is an issue within an urban community today, it is expressed in hip-hop music and culture within hours. Almost instantaneously, rap songs are created about the issue, freestyles are recited about it, tee shirts show messages that connect to it, and the entire culture is transformed. This malleable quality of hip-hop culture must be juxtaposed with the static, standardized approach to pedagogy and policy within urban science education. All too often, in these venues, contemporary issues and topics that directly affect the communities that students are a part of are notably absent from the curriculum, are never aspects of the teaching, and are never given space to be brought into science education. The static nature of urban science education contributes to the ineffectiveness of the current educational model and contributes to the active engagement of urban youth in hip-hop and their dis-engagement with science.

In my work in urban science classrooms, I have seen students unconsciously enact the communal nature of hip-hop that comes from fields where they live like talking about a topic being taught with a peer in the classroom. I have also seen them express indicators of interest like speaking along with, or overlapping speech with, a teacher and seen these behaviors being mis-identified as disrespect or rudeness. On numerous occasions, I have seen the "tag em in" process that hip-hop break dancers/b-boys engage in which involves bringing in a teammate to participate in the activity being enacted in the science classroom. Students look to assist a peer who is having a problem with answering a question or interject as a peer communicates with the teacher or moves their hands vigorously to get the teachers attention. However, these behaviors often result in the student being reprimanded for enacting what is improperly deemed as inappropriate behavior.

When the awareness is in place that the embodiment of hip-hop is not an indicator of disinterest in class, the educator has reached a new level of understanding that allows the bridge between hip-hop culture and science to become manifested in the urban classroom.

Hip-hop and Science as Different Ways of Looking at the Same World

In order to move beyond the current state of urban science education, and move towards more actively fostering effective science instruction in urban schools, an effort must be made to look at hip-hop as the ways that urban youth make sense of the world. In addition, the structural similarity between the ways they view the world and the way that scientists make sense of the world have to be explored. In this view, a more cultural view of both science and hip-hop allows the teacher and researcher to see them both as entities rooted in the schema and practices of different groups of people. This serves as another way that both science and hip-hop are inherently connected to each other.

Hip-hop breeds its creativity and its inventiveness as a result of a necessity to provide new avenues for voice to the marginalized. In the same vein, science is inherently rooted in providing new solutions to world problems. These similarities are further supported by the fact that new scientific inventions and breakthroughs continually have substantial social and economic implications on all of modern society. As a result of the responses of science to the world's problems, places across the globe are provided with advantages in fields that range from medicine to technology. However, the discipline can also be charged with being an agent that limits free thought, takes advantage of indigenous peoples and causes larger societal harms like pollution. Science as it is currently positioned stands as a proponent of closed mindedness and a "purely western" way of looking at the world. In reality, this is not fully the case and if it were the case, there would be no true way that the wealth of information received, and developed by scientists, from a range of disciplines could be so vast, innovative, informative and constantly changing. Science in itself is not a discipline that limits. The way that science has been used, the way it has been described, the history that it has inherited, and the closed-minded people who have worked to co-opt it for their own purposes have defiled the discipline. On a fundamental level, science is everywhere and can be used by all people.

In fact, I argue that part of the reason that science is often attached to the negative attributes mentioned above is not because of the flaws of the discipline, but because of the way that it is taught and the ways that it is generally presented to students in schools. Therefore, the major flaw here lies with the institutions that choose to deliver science in a rigid way that causes the discipline to appear like it is closed to openness of thought and creativity.

This reductionist process is quite similar to the way that hip-hop is perceived and associated with violence, sex, drugs or misogyny when in reality; it is not founded on, or focused on any of these attributes. This is not to say that these attributes are not found in some hip-hop music, or that there aren't scientists that are positivistic in their views of science or the world. My point is that despite their variance from the negative attributes they can be associated with, each of these cultures (science and hip-hop), are viewed in certain ways based on the stance of the person/people commenting on them. By exploring the similarities between them, we expand the discourse on hip-hop and science and bring science to the hip-hop generation.

Understanding the Exclusion of Hip-hop from Science

After a discussion on the similarities between hip-hop and science, the next step is a re-acknowledgment that science (as institutions of higher learning present it), has traditionally been closed to certain groups. This does not mean that science does not exist in spaces where these populations live, or that they do not reap the benefits of science in their lifeworlds. Aside form the Post-Sputnik argument made in the previous chapter, their exclusion from the discipline occurs because science is perceived by factions within the field of education to be a discipline that is difficult to master and set-aside only for those who are most intellectually capable of under-standing it. Consequently, populations who have been mislabeled as intellectually deficient (Blacks and Latino/as) have been in many instances purposefully steered away from science. When this purposeful steering away from science has become commonplace, institutionally supported biases that label minoritized populations as intellectually deficient function to support hip-hop's abstention from science. The display of hip-hop markers like wearing certain clothes or talking a certain way is often used as evidence that supports the notion that an urban student is not intellectually prepared for science classes (Seiler, 2005). Concurrently, participants in hip-hop have to contend with the fact that urban science education does not allow for their acceptance into science. The end result here is that students are perceived as not able to do science and are not given the opportunity to be engaged in it. Rather than focus on the flaws of schools and their personnel and their role in inhibiting the science-mindedness of urban youth, many critiques rest purely on science. This exclusive focus on the flaws of science, just like the exclusively negative focus on hip-hop, only functions to maintain rifts between students and science.

As scholars in the field of education critique "hard sciences" and critical scholars expose the subjectivity of science and the absence of plurality in the kinds of science being taught in schools, it is important to show how science, through an exploration of hip-hop's possible connections to it, can mend the rifts between participants in hip-hop and the teaching and learning of science in urban schools. The kind of science being taught to the hip-hop generation; that focuses on facts that have been developed by scientists who are far removed from them, does not work to foster the attitudes and behaviors that breed an interest in science.

Not only am I am positing that the fact-based brand of science education that currently stands does not support scientific habits of mind. I also argue that the tendency to present science as though there is a completed digital picture of science where each pixel has to be memorized, foregoes the reality that scientific knowledge, like the messages heard in hip-hop music, is always changing. Truth in science, despite the perceptions of science that students get in schools, is ever changing just as descriptions of the experiences of the marginalized are ever changing in hip-hop. West coast hip-hop, Southern hip-hop, East coast hip-hop or Australian hip-hop all share a common thread in their roots in the Bronx. However, artifacts of hip-hop like rap music, are ever evolving to give voice to a new breed of the hip-hop generation. In a sense, they are like scientific theories that evolve from existent ones and change over time.

CHAPTER 5

NEGOTIATING THE TERRAIN OF CULTURAL MISALIGNMENT

Discovering Why the Students are Silent

I AM HIP-HOP AND SCHOOL IS NOT: LYRICS, HISTORY, AND THE BLOCK

I am a product of the inner city. I come from Saturday afternoons in Brooklyn where I rode my bicycle up and down Flatbush Avenue, past Korean grocers and Jamaican restaurants, and into dreams of what it would be like to keep riding until there was no more concrete left on the sidewalks. I was always right around the corner from the rhythm of rap songs that drifted in the air, providing a soundtrack to my bike rides and my life. I lived for Italian ice, sold on street corners just feet away from hand-to-hand drug deals. I remember how licks of the ice froze my teeth just as vividly as I remember frozen faces that nodded as powder-filled vials were swept into empty pockets. I nodded back at those frozen faces and extended waves and hellos, not because they were faces of friends of mine, but because they were a part of the neighborhood and a part of my home. Those years were a perfect example of what it meant to coexist with "the other" or with others. That was and still is Brooklyn.

When my family moved to the Bronx in my early teens, my life did not change much. I still enjoyed Italian ice on Saturdays, this time on the Grand Concourse. Salsa music filled the air and often blended with rap songs from passing cars and boom boxes. Percussion from the congas of the salsa music and the drum machines of the rap music blended together and created accidental "reggaeton" before it became an official music genre. Puerto Rican flags hung from light poles and apartment windows, and flags from various Caribbean countries dangled from car mirrors and necks. Medallions swung back and forth to dancing bodies of different shapes, sizes, and shades. It was a perfect blend of varying cultures. That was and still is the Bronx.

On weekdays, I woke up early and took the train to my high school, which was in Brooklyn. It was a specialized public high school and it was about an hour and a half train ride from my family's apartment in the Bronx. Each step that I took when I walked out of my family's apartment on the fourth floor and headed to school was an experiment and mental exercise. I learned that running as I approached the stairs could enable me to jump over three more steps than if I jumped from the top of the stairs. I figured out that if I was running late, I could cut across the abandoned building across the street and shave five minutes off my walk to the train station. I quickly picked up the fact that I needed to put both straps on my knapsack before I approached the abandoned buildings because if I had to run, it would be easier if the bag were strapped tight than if it were not. I knew how to determine how far away a loud bang was in order to decide if it was safe to come outside. Through my lived experience, I learned how to methodically observe the phenomena around me and scientifically reason through them. This ability was inadvertently being honed as I went through my daily routines. It seems that to be young, Black and in the Bronx, and to overcome the scenarios with which I was constantly being presented, the building blocks of scientific reasoning (the ability to explain and predict phenomena in a rational manner relevant to the pursuit of human activity) were tools that were necessary for survival.

The Ice Grill: Forming an Identity that Responds to Society

The reasoning abilities I had developed in my youth taught me that once I headed to school on the train towards Brooklyn, I had to pull my baseball cap further down my forehead and over my eyes, pull my pants a little lower, clench my fists a little tighter and wear a menacing scowl. The scowl on my face was called the "ice grill" and it became so much of a part of who my friends and I were, that it was almost like a piece of clothing that we wore. In any adverse situation, we would put on our ice grill to shield us from the eyes of those who viewed us as worthless just as quickly as we would throw on a baseball cap or a jacket to shield us from the cold of a New York winter. The menacing ice grill would stay on our faces for as long as it took for the world around us to recognize our presence and acknowledge our strength. Certain situations allowed the ice grill to melt while others only kept it frozen on our faces for a lot longer than needed. The deciding factor on whether to wear the ice-grill was always the reception we got from the people around us. If they were hip-hop, like we were, we could tell. A slight head nod or a demure smile would tell their story because it meant that it was similar to ours. Anything different meant they were not on our side and deserved the menacing stares we gave them.

I would meet my friends at certain train stops along the way to Brooklyn and we would give each other our almost three minute handshakes when we saw each other. We would then collectively pull all our feelings of camaraderie together to show our collective anger at the world through the looks on our faces. The ice grill instilled fear in older folks and people from other neighborhoods, and when my friends and I wore it, people clenched purses tighter and avoided making eye contact with us. We would hold the looks on our faces tightly until the train had traveled through Manhattan and we were at a train stop in Brooklyn that felt like home. From the looks on the faces of the older people who wore business suits and exited the trains in Manhattan, I knew there was a consensus that our attire and demeanor meant we were bound for a life of failure and regret. For some, it meant we were people to be feared. To others, we were just another group of young Black males with a scripted and bleak future. To my friends and I, our projected image meant we were thinking a little harder, were a little bit sharper, and a were a little more prepared than anyone else for any surprises life offered. We were hip-hop.

By the time my friends and I got deep enough into Brooklyn, the trains emptied and our faces would relax. We sat across from each other, discussing the newest rap songs that were out, created freestyle rap about our lives, banged on the seats of the train to create rap beats, and talked about sports and life in general.

As soon as we got off the train and headed towards school, the ice grill re-emerged. Mine remained on my face as I walked through the school building and into my classes, and was particularly frozen on my face as I maneuvered through the hallways and into my science classes. In those fields, I sat and listened to the teacher speak, wanting to be a part of the discussions, hoping to share my ideas, but feeling as though what was going on was completely removed from who I was and who people like me were. As the school day ended, and I got closer to my neighborhood, I slowly became myself again. I straightened my hat, unclenched my fists, and allowed the ice grill to melt.

From the Ice Grill to Science Achievement: Exploring the Connections

In urban schools, there are millions of students of color who wear the ice grill and are a part of hip-hop. They navigate the terrain of their everyday worlds, walk into schools, and travel through science classrooms prepared for surviving in the world outside of the classroom while they remain unprepared for success within their classrooms. The statistics to support this point loom upon science educators and researchers and call for a focus on revamping current efforts to move students of color in urban settings towards science. Rodriguez (1997) discusses the wide achievement gaps between minority and White students in science, and NCES (2006) data are consistent with this finding. Concurrently, the Council of Graduate Schools reports that the percentages of African American and Hispanic students who receive college degrees in the sciences are disproportionately low in comparison to their White counterparts (CGS, 2009). In New York State, it has been reported that Black and Latino/Latina students in urban schools who happen to be the populations who create, and are mostly a part of hip-hop, take fewer science classes and perform worse on standardized science exams than do their peers in other schools (NYSED, 2007). In the Bronx, the birthplace of hip-hop and the site of much of my research, students score 20% lower than their peers on the New York City assessments in science (nycenet.edu, 2007). However, the most telling statistic for me is evident when I peer through classroom doors, sit in the back of classes, or teach physics and chemistry in urban science classrooms, and see hundreds of students displaying the ice grill in their science classes.

Barton and Yang (2000) documented the realities of poorer and fewer resources, more inexperienced teachers, and lower funding in urban schools when compared to suburban schools. These factors are instrumental to the lower achievement of Black and Latino/Latina youth in science and need to be addressed. However, I argue that these factors cannot be solely responsible for urban students' poor achievement. The issues that plague urban science education are bigger than the established causes for low achievement and are rooted in the differences between the culture of the traditional science teacher and that of the student.

Most people who have an interest in urban education, such as educational researchers who focus on achievement gaps in science, support the assertion that cultural misalignments play some role in achievement gaps. While it is not politically correct to blame urban youth for their academic struggles or be outright in representing urban youth as disinterested in education and unwilling to learn, there are many entities within education that covertly take this stance through their focus on cultural misalignments. Any substantial time spent in the teachers' lounge in urban schools affirms this fact as teachers readily share their negative and oftentimes racially biased perceptions of students with each other. Many who do not blame urban youth for their academic struggles, do inadvertently blame parents and certain racial or ethnic groups as a whole for being reluctant to take advantage of the educational opportunities presented to them.

For researchers who buy into these ways of thinking, who either covertly or overtly blame hip-hop youth and their parents for urban students of color's disconnection from the science classroom, the exhibition of the ice grill in the science class is seen as a conscious choice not to be involved in classroom learning. In some instances, it is also seen as a form of empty posturing that is part of hip-hop and exhibited without cause. In fields beyond the classroom, the exhibition of this part of one's hip-hopness is misperceived as empty or blind anger. I argue that it is an exhibition of the hip-hop generations' commitment to realness and unpretentiousness and a defense mechanism. There is a necessary realness or honesty that causes the participant in hip-hop to express discontent when it is felt, and show a visible and outright response to even subtle messages by those outsiders of their culture that they are not valued or accepted. In fields like urban classrooms, teachers often categorize a student as being "angry" or a "problem child" without an understanding that the behavior the student exhibits, is a response to the structures of the school and is an attempt to be honest or "real" with his or her dissatisfaction with the classroom.

By reflecting on my past experiences as an urban student, and closely analyzing my observations of the urban youth I work with, I find that if more attention is focused on the experiences of urban youth outside of the school and the policies that may cause the exhibition of disinterest in school, reasons for the exhibition of the ice-grill become apparent. This approach aligns with Comer's (1996) view that involves a holistic look at urban youth, and educating the entire urban child emotionally and intellectually. My approach extends beyond this work by identifying their allegiance to hip-hop as a fundamental piece of who they are and the chief tool through which urban youth connect to school and science. Furthermore, my work explores the hip-hop identity that students in urban settings more fully embody as they spend more years in urban schools. I find that the longer students spend in urban schools that do not validate them, the more aggressive and disinterested they become. As time within schools pass by, a permanent ice grill slowly forms. I argue that if one could follow the prototypical urban student from the 3rd grade to the tenth grade (when most high school dropouts leave school), one could trace the history of how a third grader's smile slowly forms into a menacing scowl.

Melting the Ice Grill

Throughout my teaching and learning experiences in urban settings, I have found that no specific strand of thought can quantify the complexities of teaching and learning science without a focus on democracy. Even the most important arguments for improving science education, such as a more constructivist approach to science instruction, has proven to be ineffectual when it does not consider democracy – or the involvement of all students in the classroom (Bencze, 2000). By this, I mean that we cannot claim to value how students make sense of the world, if we do not allow for the expression of their out of school knowledge. Approaching a way to address the educational inequities that exist in urban schools without a contextual investigation of the social fields that impact teaching and learning, and the role of the students in these fields, is categorically undemocratic.

When I walk into the classroom, I walk in believing that all students have an equal voice in working to address the inequities that exist in the classroom. I walk into classrooms believing that students have the same voice in the classroom that they have in hip-hop. My work in addressing academic or behavior issues within the science classroom is not rooted in conferring of a cause or solution to the problems I face, but is a joint discovery of solutions with hip-hop youth through a lens that considers their ways of making sense of the world.

If the teacher or researcher values the culture of all participants, and perceives all that they bring to the classroom as being valuable for understanding what is going on in the classroom, the "ice grill" on students' faces would not be seen as unjustified angst towards science or schooling but as the physical manifestation of feeling powerless and the expression of emotion in response to this powerlessness. Hooks (2004) describes the hyper-vigilance of Black people in response to the trauma of daily oppression resulting in their expression of a constant guarded stance. I argue that this hyper-vigilance is where the cold and stern looks and attitudes that students exhibit in science classrooms originate. The ice-grill is formed by the need to create a facade of brute strength and is a significant piece of hip-hop. This facade functions to conceal vulnerability even though it is expressed as a mask of disinterest. The ice grill in the science classroom functions to obscure wonder and curiosity, but is actually a means to hide disappointment in not being able to actively participate.

FOLLOWING THE LYRICS TO THE PROMISE LAND

As I began to look past ice grills, and study participants in hip-hop and their experiences in science classrooms, I created a chart of hip-hop lyrics to organize my thoughts. The chart began with a single lyric from the Notorious B.I.G. where he dedicated his album to the teachers who told him he wouldn't amount to anything and eventually grew into a notebook full of lyrics and phrases that are directly related to school and science. By just listening to the radio and paying attention to lyrics that the students were reciting, I collected thousands of verses from rap songs that provided deep insight into the hip-hop generations' view of schools. As I began to analyze these lyrics, I would write them down, describe the context surrounding a particular lyric, and ask students about what the words the artists were saying meant to them. The song lyrics then became an entry point for profound conversations about what they thought of schools.

Each time I met with a group of students to have these discussions, their words reminded me that they were experiencing scenarios that were similar to the ones that I had when I was in their shoes decades ago. They identified with the lyrics, understood the contexts surrounding rap artists' frustration with school, and echoed a sentiment that teaching a new way was necessary. After our conversations, I began to observe the students more closely and tried to connect the lyrics we had listened to, to their classroom behaviors. In many instances, I would see them reciting rap lyrics under their breath and wearing ice grills in their science classes. They would not only recite the lines I shared with them that mentioned school and science, but others that discussed other scenarios like police brutality or poverty where voices were silenced. It was evident that the marriage between hip-hop and the urban student was alive and manifested daily.

Married Hip Hop and Divorcing School Science

After my short study based on rap lyrics, I delved into my personal collection of rap music to conduct a quick study. I began by scrolling through my digital music player and listening to a pool of rap songs, focusing specifically on how they may relate to schools. I quickly realized that many more rap songs than I expected focused on broader issues of racism and oppression, inequities in society at large, and the experiences of students who are marginalized from attainment in schools. However, the more I listened to, and attempted to deconstruct these lyrics, the more I realized that there were many issues related to the relationship between hip-hop and school science that I had not previously considered.

The focus on evidence from everyday life being significant for teaching science, the authority given to scientists by the scientifically literate public, and even the arguments about what is considered science within the field of science (Chalmers, 1999) align with how rappers base their lyrics on real life experiences, how they are given the authority to speak for participants in hip-hop, and arguments about what is real hip-hop and what isn't (Quinn, 2005). The result of fully immersing myself in rap lyrics was that I came to more fully understand their significance to school and science. In addition, listening to rap lyrics on a daily basis challenged me to continue with explorations of how to understand and improve the experiences of a urban youth who are married to hip-hop and ostracized from society and schools.

Rapper Joe Buddens describes this marriage to hip-hop in a lyric that states "I married hip-hop, ignored what some were telling me" (Buddens, 2007). He then proceeds to mention how he could never divorce her (hip-hop). This description of hip-hop as a life partner by participants in the culture and the love and respect of hip-hop that is a theme of much rap music by artists like the Roots and Common who have songs solely dedicated to their love affair with hip-hop, stand in sharp contradiction to the negative themes found in other rap lyrics.

While the scope of the discussion about negative rap lyrics and the off color themes of certain rap songs are outside of the frame of this study, I do acknowledge that the negative themes that appear in hip-hop are problematic and need to be addressed. Despite this need, it is important to recognize that the description of these rap lyrics, as the picture of hip-hop or as a representation of hip-hop culture is a gross overrepresentation of a miniscule part of the lives and experiences of those who are immersed in it. The power of being so tied to hip-hop that one would never leave it stands as a staunch contradiction to the fact that urban youth become so divorced from school that they constantly look for opportunities to escape from its confines. Lyrics like Joe Buddens' and his pride in a marriage to hip-hop plays starkly against the words of students who end up proud of being divorced from school. These students sit in the back of the classroom with their heads down, intentionally disrupt the classroom, and wear their ice grill in order to show that they are divorced from what is going on in the classroom.

These are the students that express brilliance when they are engaged in hip-hop, but require an extra effort to connect to school and science. In my work, I sit with them both inside and outside of the classroom, show an interest in where they come from, and invite them to engage in conversations with me about the potential of connecting hip-hop and school. Each time that I engage in this process, their disinterest in school turns into excitement as they discuss hip hop and its possible connections to their experiences in school. When I have invited teachers to be a part of these conversations, the level of excitement and passion the students exhibit have made teachers wonder if they were talking with the same students who have refused to take off their baseball caps in the classroom, or who in one instance said "f— this class" with all the hate and disgust those three words can muster.

Interrogating the words and worlds of these students to find out why they are married to hip-hop and divorced from school reveals the beauty of their culture and its difference from the restrictions of the science classroom. These conversations echoed themes that I found in hip-hop music that mention schools and spanned many topics within the field of education. Words like dropout, teachers, school, diploma, degree, G.E.D, homework, high school, scholar, class, and graduate repetitively surfaced in both conversations with students and studies of rap lyrics.

While the contexts surrounding the use of these words were sometimes negative, the information that came from them was always valuable. In rap lyrics, I would hear lines like "I'm the dropout that made more money than these teachers" (50 cent, 2004), "I'm the proud new owner of the [New Jersey] Nets, no diploma no regrets" (Jay Z, 2005), "I make a lot of zeroes, that's what my teachers called me, predictions like they're Cleo" (D.J. Unk, 2007). In these lyrics, I heard hip-hop participants valuing themselves for what they have achieved and throwing their success in the face of their former teachers. These lyrics were the actions of the students in urban classrooms put to music.

In other lyrics, I heard stories about students' experiences within schools or within higher education and the realities of the lives of hip-hop participants. Lyrics like "Ain't no diploma or degrees, but you can get high from the aroma of the trees" and "No Sesame Street kids watch BET, look up to niggas who don't got a G.E.D." (Fabolous, 2006) served as introductions into the feelings of the urban student towards schooling. I heard frustration with the structures of schools that resulted in either harsh critique of schools or an affirmation of oneself as outside of the norms of schools. Lyrics like, "I was a terror since the public school era" (Notorious B.I.G., 2004) displayed the fact that the embodiment of being a "terror" did not begin when a person was at home, but began with an interaction with urban public schools. Other lyrics like "These are our heroes, thanks a lot, public school system still rots, still runnin from cops" (Nas, 2006) targeted the dysfunction of the urban public school and the absence of heroes or models within such institutions. Even more profound than these lyrics and the themes they discuss is the existence of a hip-hop created schooling system that is an alternate to the urban public school.

The hip-hop school is different from traditional urban educational systems with teachers that are non-representative of, and disinterested in the culture of hip-hop participants. In the hip-hop school, rappers are seen as scholars or educators. Many rappers refer to the "School of Hard Knocks," a term describing the streets of the inner city, as where they got their education. Furthermore, rappers state proudly that they are scholars without a diploma no G.E.D. (T.I., 2005) who are grown men because they are "not in school" (Mos Def, 2004). They let formal institutions know that they are educating urban youth, whether or not society or schools like it (Rass Kass, 1997), and they wear their ice grills proudly to show that they have value that lies beyond the formal schooling institutions that do not accept them.

Since they are part of an educational system that holds different values than the traditional school, many artists speak about the fact that they believe that what they are taught in formal schools are lies that do not mean anything in the real world. I often hear rappers say that they've felt like fools when they have tried to learn in schools because only science and math in the real world (and not taught within schools) are truly universal (Cee Lo Green, 2000). Others wonder how hip-hop exists through the facts, written in school textbooks, because they are not true reflections of the hip-hop generation (Nas, 1994).

Lyrics where rappers talk about being products of the projects, and considered by teachers to be rejects (Jim Jones, 2005), or when they dedicate their work to teachers that "told them that they would never amount to nothin" (Notorious B.I.G., 1994) suggest that students are not valued in school and paints the picture of the realities of urban school culture where students are perceived as valueless.

The sentiments expressed in these lyrics echo the words described by the urban youth that I have conducted research with. My research with them indicates that the overwhelming effort required to live through challenging everyday situations makes it particularly challenging for urban youth to cross the barriers of a cultural divide between school science and everyday life. The conscious separation between students and schools perpetuated by the school and reaffirmed by the rapper tarnishes the reputations of each group in the eyes of the other.

As time goes by, and tarnished reputations continue to build barriers, the gaps between participants in hip-hop and schools continue to widen. In the case of school science, the divides between participants in hip-hop and science widens even further because of science's stance as the discipline that is least willing to amend itself to the needs of a population not historically represented in it. In fact, science in urban schools is often closely partnered with a western history that focuses on the accomplishments and inventions of scientists that do not reflect the ethnic, racial or gender demographics of students in urban schools. In order to delve more deeply into the separation of hip-hop from science, I interject our current line of analysis for a brief re-introduction to hip-hop that specifically focuses on the hip-hop generation. This segue serves to ground the work as I transition into more thorough analysis of the hip-hop participants' troubled relationship with urban science education.

Who is Hip-hop? The Makings of a Hip-hop Student

The population that makes up the original hip-hop generation has been described as those born between 1964 and 1984 (Kitwana, 2002). I argue that this timeline should be modified to include people born both before and after that time block. Those within the age group that Kitwana describes can be considered the anchor of the hip-hop generation because the timeline of their existences parallels the advent of hip-hop as a cultural phenomenon. However, the inclusionary nature of the culture allows for those born before that time and those born after that era to become pulled into the culture. The nature of hip-hop, and the way that it allows individuals from various backgrounds to develop the schema and practices necessary for immersion into it, allows for the extension of the age bracket previously given to the hip-hop generation.

Urban youth that I have taught and conducted research with, that were born in the mid 1990's, are as fully engulfed in the culture as those within the 1964–1984 timeframe. This occurs because the communitarian way of thought that is inherent in hip-hop supports the argument that a person's identity with one's community is the principal or dominant (perhaps even the only significant) identity a person has (Sen, 2006). Therefore, being born into a hip-hop community oftentimes almost forces a person into being a part of hip-hop culture.

I have seen three year olds stumble over the words to rap lyrics and mic (microphone) check with their rattles as they are unconsciously brought into a world where their identities as hip-hop youth are already inscribed. Unfortunately, these children are inevitably positioned as unable to learn and be a part of science because they are part of the hip-hop generation.

As hip-hop has emerged as a culture of its own, replete with varying dialects, beliefs, morals, art and traditions, it has reached deeper than any ethnic inscriptions attributed to Black or Latino/a youth. Its presence as an avenue of voice for the marginalized across the globe has made it a cultural understanding for many. As such, the global scope of hip-hop has to be utilized as a tool for redesigning science curricula that is intended to provide voice for populations that traditionally are not a part of science.

Marginalized populations across the globe have had a chance to witness the ways that hip-hop has provided voice for urban minority youth in the United States. Consequently, they have adopted hip-hop into their local cultural understandings and ways of communicating. In an edited book that explores hip-hop in Europe, Anglophone and Francophone Canada, Japan, and Australia, Mitchell (2001) features authors who interrogate hip-hop in these different places and outlines the feeling of being ostracized from mainstream culture that is a thread in hip-hop across these contexts. Through hip-hop, we are able to see what Forman (2002) describes as Nancy Fraser's (1992) conception of "subaltern counterpublics."

Forman presents hip-hop as inhabiting spaces where the negotiation between domination and subordination are in constant flux. In this description, it stands as a field where populations develop the agency to subvert the authority of those who have power through their involvement in a space where they can exchange thoughts and ideas and counter domination. Hip-hop serves as a counter-public space that is readily accessible by all who look to transference from a presently oppressive state. It stands in opposition to established public spaces that alienate and marginalize certain people, and connects the marginalized within these spaces to each other. If a student within a classroom feels ostracized from discourse within a social field like the science classroom, rather than push to exchange within that classroom, she turns towards hip-hop as an avenue to describe the feeling of being ostracized.

It can be argued that there are multiple definitions of science, and different ways that science makes sense to different people. These definitions are described by Derry (1999) as the view that takes science as the sum of all facts in all science textbooks, and the other that takes science as the endless methods of instruction, and ways of thinking that go beyond fact and results. These divergent strands of science create arguments within the field between those that see science as a constant search for information in an expanding and evolving world, and those that see science as understanding a pre-established picture of the world. Generally, contemporary scientists takes the latter stance. As such, science as it is mostly understood by scientists (and not science teachers), is connected to hip-hop in yet another way.

Because hip-hop is not a physical or geographic space with parameters or boundaries, but a symbolic space that can be entered through various means, many enter into it by bringing their struggles within the specific social fields that oppress them. When Nas describes "…his mind in a another world, wondering how do we exist through the facts written in school textbooks" (Nas, 1994) he not only describes his struggles with making sense of school, but an entry into another world (hip-hop) that can be accessed by others who wonder how they exist through the harsh realities of their own specific conditions. In this other world, the power to act is provided to all participants, and they can use this power to escape their realities.

When a person is aware that she has the power to act, she eagerly awaits opportunities to exercise this power in the creation of a foreseeable new future. Hip-hop then becomes the immediate alternative to, or means of expressing agency in response to, any oppressive scenario. I have seen this when students whistle the tune to a rap song in class where a teacher is always yelling, murmur lyrics to a song under their breath during an exam, or change their dispositions in a matter of seconds when they feel threatened by something that the teacher says, or when they throw on their ice grill in response to a particular scenario in class.

The Anti-science Labeling of the Hip-hop Student

Science teachers who see the students' enactment of agency as a response to the structures of the classroom interact differently with students than those who do not see this connection. Furthermore, how the teacher conceives of science, and who is a part of science, determines what science becomes when it is taught in the classroom. If science is perceived as a stoic, fact laden and non-experiential discipline, any group of people who view themselves as full of emotion or passionate, and/or focused on real world experiences become other than science. Furthermore, if the teacher perceives her identity as tied to science and also has a part of her identity nested in a culture that is anti hip-hop, then she will perceive anything outside of her norms or the spaces she inhabits, as other than herself and other than science. The tying of the teacher's identity to science, and the perception of the expression of a hip-hop identity as other than science places students in opposition to science even before they get an opportunity to express an interest in the discipline.

I argue that this positioning of the urban student as not a part of science or anti-science forces the student to enact practices or behaviors that indicate a disregard the discipline. This reaction is the same one that participants in hip-hop take in response to any oppression in society and results in urban youths' non-involvement in established social systems like the political or school system. Science teachers, who view themselves as having a certain type of intelligence, class, stature, or position that ties them to science, have their own lifeworlds. These vary from hip-hop youth lifeworlds because they involve a deep involvement in established social systems and norms that are against hip-hop youth.

Greene (1995) makes many arguments for educational researchers/teachers to move beyond the confines of their self-created worlds. She calls for a viewing of spaces that impact school and schooling as part of the process of teaching in, and researching schools. Using this argument as a springboard, I present hip-hop as one of the most significant spaces that affects school, and a necessary lifeworld that teachers of marginalized populations must enter, and attempt to understand. With the acceptance of hip-hop as a significant space for exploration by teachers of marginalized students comes a need to move beyond the traditional conceptions of what the culture entails. For the teacher, it becomes necessary to embrace hip-hop and not view participants in it as subjects (both in the sense of undergoing a treatment of schooling and as under the rule of the teacher). Rather they must be seen as the ambassadors of hip-hop culture and experts in an area where the teacher is a novice.

The Researchers Role in the Anti-science Labeling of Hip-hop Participants

In addressing the role of researchers in the anti-science labeling of the urban student, I begin with a focus on the hip-hop student as subject and on the term "human subject research" that has been inherited by educational research from research in fields beyond it. I also focus on who is perceived as the research subject and what is meant by subject in the kind of work that focuses on urban youth in science education. My questioning of this notion is tied to my experiences in conducting research in science classrooms. It is also based on my readings of scholarly work in science education that seems to be working towards understanding the issues of non-achievement in science of urban youth, but inadvertently works towards a presentation of these populations as subjects – to be saved and rescued from their disinterest in school and science. In much of this type of work, the presentation of the data resources display a simple re-verification of perceptions of urban youth without an investigation of their experiences or an understanding of their hip-hop culture. This is not to say that science education research in urban settings is riddled with blatant unethical practice. In fact, over the course of the last few years, researchers have worked towards showing evidence of increased science knowledge among students of color without leaning towards an approach that looks to save the urban student from themselves. However, on a more grand scale, science education research done in urban settings foregoes the understandings of the complex worlds of participants, completely ignores any relationships to hip-hop, and describes characteristics that can be linked to populations in urban settings without attempting to understand their relation to students' culture.

Perceptions of Urban Youth in Urban Education Research

As alluded to earlier, expanding science education research to include the experiences of those most marginalized from it requires an awareness of the schematic understandings that the researcher/teacher brings to the classroom. These understandings often manifest themselves as deficit-based perspectives of urban youth, where they are seen as participants in research that have issues that only the researcher can address or describe. As the conventional scenario is played out in urban education research, when a researcher engages in a study with students in urban schools, there is a description or identity that urban students have been given that they have little to no ability to move from. In this process, the larger achievement gaps that exist between urban students and their counterparts in other settings are automatically deduced to be a function of the inability of urban youth. Usually, some observations are made of the student, a treatment is implemented to address an issue that has been observed, and the researcher expresses surprise when a student does something positive like explain a concept clearly, give a correct answer, or understand a scientific idea/concept/principle. The study is then presented in the conventional scholarly manner and distributed to other scholars within the field. This model's enforcing of negative perceptions of urban youth is a constant issue that is masked by the fact that this type of research is presented as though it is helping urban youth.

When this type of research is presented to students who are from the populations where urban science education research is conducted, the model of research and the products of such work have profound effects on the students' perceptions of themselves and what they feel they can do or are expected to do in science. In a research group that consisted of three students that classified themselves as hip-hop youth, I presented a number of research articles about urban schools and urban science education and asked them to share their opinions about the articles. The resulting discussion resulted in students' discussions about feeling as though they were being described as unable to achieve in science because of their backgrounds. Two of the students were participants in a "metalogue" where they expressed a view that the messages being put forth by the scholarly work in urban science education in the work they looked at only served as a means to further pigeon hole students from urban schools into a group of students that are unable to achieve in science (Emdin, 2007a). I argue that these deficit perspectives are fortified by the associations made between the research subjects (particularly research subjects of color in urban schools) and their inability to be successful in school before they receive a treatment of some type that is provided by the researcher. In the process of describing the experiences of marginalized urban youth, they are often inadvertently described as being less than the researcher. They are not expected to be able to question research products or teaching practices, suggest research questions, topics to be covered in class, or engage in research/ teaching on their own. There is a collective dismissal of their understandings and abilities and this researcher stance only serves as further reasons why they collectively reject an acceptance of school and schooling. The urban science students' association with a community of low achievement functions in tandem with all the negative generalizations that come with being a part of that community. This combines with the symbolic tag of research subject that is placed on these populations by researchers who oftentimes support a culture that views hip-hop participants as the underbelly of any "civilized" society.

As we proceed, I present and describe the tenets of hip-hop and how they may be used to support teachers and researchers whose work in science education is dedicated to bridging the inequities in the teaching and learning of science for marginalized populations. The use of these tools has the potential to help researchers move towards attaining ethical research practices and understanding the lives of the populations they do research with-who are a part of the hip-hop culture.

Hip Hop's Ancestry

In previous work, I have discussed how people have historically treated one another with respect and civility or a profound lack thereof. I have also discussed how either stance affects our present understandings of each other and the ways we presently conduct research (Emdin & Lehner, 2007). In other words, our collective understandings of what is acceptable, or who is deserving of our respect, have roots in norms that have been established by those before us. Accounts of history get translated over generations, become interpreted and reinforced through the lenses of those who have power, and become rooted in a present population's fundamental understandings of others. This fact explains the complex relationships between teachers/ researchers and hip-hop and also provides insight into how to address the various issues with teaching and learning of science that arise from these relationships.

Historically, teachers of Black students and new immigrants have always equated the teaching of these populations with training them to fit into an established mold of what it is to be "American" or "civil." Tyack & Cuban, (1995) has described that historically, the teaching of immigrant populations in the United States involves an "Americanizing" of these populations. As a collective, Black Americans, who have historically not received respect or civility in the United States, have been presented and treated as a population not deserving of being a part of mainstream America or unable to be completely Americanized. This was (and in some cases still is) the case because they respond to the inability to be completely American by embracing more local cultures that they feel are more strong pieces of their identity, and more accurate representatives of who they are.

Responses to forms of oppression like slavery and other struggles of African Americans in the United States have always been vividly expressed in places of worship like the Black church. In these spaces their responses to not being seen as American and being different from mainstream America are brilliantly expressed through song and preaching. In these spaces, the oppressed have the opportunity to let down their guards and transform themselves into places where the inequities and injustices that they experience outside of their places of worship are temporarily non-existent. Historically, membership in the Black church was an open call to all Blacks, and the church became a part of their culture.

For hip-hop participants, the history of being disrespected or not treated civilly is partly inherited through this part of Black American history. I argue that hip-hop's modes of expression are evolutions of the narrative and song of the Black church. As slaves used their autobiographies as means to demonstrate the deep effects of the degradation of the souls of their ancestors, their selves and their offspring (Gates, 1991), hip-hop artists speak for those within their communities that lack the voice to express their degradation.

On the song "Hard Knock Life," Jay-Z (1998), who is a world-renowned rapper, begins the second verse saying that he speaks for those lost because of drugs and who are incarcerated. On the song, he mentions that he raps in the memory of slain rapper Notorious B.I.G. and demonstrates the need for those who have voice to speak or write to ensure that they speak for all those who do not and cannot speak for themselves. On this song, he expresses a key attribute of hip-hop and explains the hip-hop audience's connection to the rap artist. He also demonstrates how the rapper speaks for the community. This speaking for others that is found in rap occurs because of an inherent need of the hip-hop community to be responsible for all those who are marginalized as a part of the Black-American tradition. The need to be responsible for one another is one of the deep tenets of hip-hop and connects deeply to the philosophical tenet of cosmopolitanism and the concept of a responsibility for the other that is at its root (Appiah, 2006, Breckenridge, Pollock, Bhabha, & Chakrabarty, 2002). It also ties into the understanding that the cosmopolitan acts of hip-hop's forefathers, expressed through the profound autobiographies of the slave, are the root from which new forms of cosmopolitan discourse in current hip-hop is expressed. Indeed, "the new must be made precisely through attachment to the past, and by recognizing that only such attachment enables one to grasp what can and must be changed" (Pollock, 2000, p).

The cosmopolitan roots of hip-hop are part of the same way of knowing as slave narratives and church preaching. Like hip-hop, in these spaces a single person or group of people can express their experiences and that of their kin. The cosmopolitan nature of hip-hop includes people from backgrounds other than Black American and makes it clear that in hip-hop, one's kin are not just those related by blood but those related by experience. This is particularly the case if the shared experience is oppression at the hands of the same institutions and the same political and social economies that exclude certain people from fully participating in the activities within a particular social field. Within hip-hop, these populations begin to share the same language, understandings and dispositions and begin to define what is good, fair and equitable from their position as the marginalized.

The Researcher's Role in Silencing the Hip-hop Generation

As the continual formation and re-formation of collective understandings takes place within the hip-hop community, researchers continue to make judgments about goodness, fairness, and equity based on generalized notions of these attributes that they form without input from those they want to do good by who hold their own definitions. This is partly the case because the marginalized in urban settings are a part of hip-hop, and hip-hop is not acknowledged as a bloc with its own genuine and distinct understandings. The researcher inherits traditions about what it means to conduct research and be equitable that is tainted by perceptions of who the researcher is, and who the researched should be. In instances where the identities of urban youth are taken into consideration, a focus may be on specific racial or ethnic groups, without the consideration that they are all a part of a hip-hop generation that has shared understandings. Generalized notions of the researcher take the form of the period's dominant ideology which inevitably involves a demarcation between who the researcher is and who the researcher is doing research on. In this system, some forms of knowledge are affirmed while others are subjugated and hip-hop culture is not considered as encompassing any necessary knowledge.

In urban science education research, these issues have not been deeply examined and consequently, the urban student is not accurately described or understood. Though not necessarily a deliberate ethical misadventure, the very exclusion of an authentic part of the lives of those being studied does pose an ethical dilemma. This is not to say that all researchers are inherently unethical. However, it is apparent that there is a domain that has been ignored and needs to be investigated. If the ways research products are presented, and the descriptions of the students in the research do not reflect what the hip-hop generation considers as part of their culture, there is an issue with the authenticity of the research. Furthermore, if the responsibility for each other that the participants in hip-hop share with each other is not reflected in the research, it is not truly representative of the populations that it theoretically hopes to benefit.

As time passes, if the subjugated knowledges from either literally or meta-phorically colonized communities like hip-hop are inhibited from finding their ways into mainstream discourse, the research community ends up being a force that functions to silence the student. In the case of hip-hop, globalization has allowed for the voice of hip-hop participants across the globe to become heard even when research in urban schools has silenced it. Through the worldwide distribution of hip-hop, previously silenced voices speak loudly and are internationally recognized. They simply await the research community to evolve with the times and become aware of their existence.

BLAME AND POWER IN URBAN SCIENCE EDUCATION

PLAYING THE BLAME GAME

It was the last day of school after my first year of teaching and I was excited that I had finally made it through the year. The last few students had left the school building and as is customary in some New York City public schools, I waited with some fellow teachers by the principal's office waiting for our summer pay and a copy of our final observations. While I was excited about the pay I was about to receive, I was more excited about how I would be assessed by the Principal. I had some struggles with classroom management, had not planned some lessons the exact way I was supposed to, and had many other challenges as the year progressed. Although I feel like I made some genuine connections with students, and made sure that they learned something, I wasn't quite sure how I would be assessed.

My name was finally called to enter the office and I sat at the chair in front of the principal's desk. The minute I sat down, I felt like I was back in junior high school. Sweat formed on my brow and my palms became moist. I rubbed my hands together and looked up at the principal as he pulled a long sheet of paper from his desk. He asked me how I felt I had done as a teacher during the academic year, and I wasn't quite sure how to respond. I thought of my successes and also some of my struggles and for a second did not know what to say. I decided to respond honestly and say that I was not so sure. He responded by saying that he knew I should have had more support. He then said, "things get hectic when you're dealing with these types of kids."

As soon as I realized where he was going with the conversation, I joined him. I mentioned how tough it was to teach the students from the housing projects. I mentioned a situation where a student pulled a fire alarm in the hallway when I was trying to teach, and he responded with another story about a fight in the staircase. Before I even realized it, we had begun to engage in a game of who could tell the worst story about the students. As we spoke, he grabbed a pen from a cup on the table, and began to fill in my observation form. It seemed as if the more we spoke, the more his pen danced across the paper. Before long, he looked up at me, handed me my formal observation, and congratulated me on a successful academic year. There were parts of the observation sheet that asked about classroom management, preparation of assignments, and delivery of lessons that were all marked satisfactory or even excellent when I knew that at times, these were points where I was deficient.

As I walked out of the office, I was filled with elation. I had successfully completed the school year. As I think back on that experience, I realize that I had not received any assistance from my school administrator or the education class I had taken at a local college. However, it seemed that as long as the students were to blame, or as long as I didn't blame the school administration or the school, everything was okay.

In many of the conversations surrounding the effectiveness of teaching science in urban schools, much blame is placed on different groups for the reasons why instruction is ineffective and achievement is low. The blame is always directed to a specific other group in an attempt to obtain absolution from any responsibility for the problems that plague urban education. Oftentimes, those who have the least agency in affecting change (urban youth who are a part of hip-hop) are blamed for low achievement and are presented to the general populace as a picture of what non-achievement looks like. In some instances, the belief that hip-hop is connected to non-achievement causes bans on hip-hop or even on what is considered hip-hop clothing in schools. The blame that is placed on hip-hop for having a generally negative influence on urban youth includes its blame for being a cause for both poor student interest and achievement in school. Ferguson, (2001) attempted to chart the rise of hip-hop music with increasing rates of poor educational achieve- ment, and McWhorter (2003) railed against rap and described hip-hop as a pheno- menon that holds back Blacks in America.

These discussions about the negative effects of hip-hop are a piece of a larger phenomenon that involves the positioning of anything other than established ways of understanding as counterproductive to learning. I argue that these hypercritical, largely unfounded, and generally mean-spirited critiques of rap and hip-hop show that "if it were left to academic discourse, we would continually be reduced by a shallow and limited analysis offered as the fact of our (African American/ marginalized populations) creative work" (Banfield, 2004, p. 99). This shallow analysis/critique of rap breeds negative perceptions about hip-hop culture among those who are not a part of it and fosters hip-hop's extraction from educational discourse. This extraction of hip-hop then causes the discourse on urban education to be unreflective of the reality of students' experiences.

The inability of the critiques of hip-hop to garner much traction within the fields where hip-hop is created, while they garner attention by those who are outside of hip-hop, is another point that is reflective of the divergent perspectives of those involved in the culture and those outside of it. Furthermore, the inability of groups interested in education to fully and clearly tie hip-hop to the societal ills it is blamed for shows tremendous weakness in the argument that hip-hop is inherently bad for urban youth and their education.

The results of the inability to directly blame hip-hop for the flaws in schools, and the effects of not being able to generate the same sort of prejudicial fear of "the other" in regards to hip-hop within education, results in a continued effort to find some entity to blame for non-achievement in urban schools. In many instances, schools of education focus their blame on the bureaucracies that govern schools who, in turn, place blame back on schools of education. Within schools, admini- strators often place the blame for low achievement on teachers. In response, teachers look to the schools of education that are supposed to prepare them for teaching.

In an online group that I coordinated among first year science teachers across New York City, they repeatedly cited poor preparation for the realities of urban schools as a reason for their struggles. These teachers noted a separation between what they learned about teaching in schools of education from what they needed to succeed as teachers in these schools. These types of complaints strike a harsh blow to departments in academic institutions that pride themselves on their effective teacher preparation. As a result, schools of education engage in another phase of the blame game where they tie in various other issues to explain the lack of success of urban schools. These include circumstances such as the hyper focus on classroom testing as a result of the No Child Left Behind Act, and poorly designed curriculum, or poor implementation of it.

As conversations about where the root of the issues in urban science classrooms progress, representatives of each faction within education almost unanimously maintain that they are not to blame and do so vocally through teacher and administrator unions, governmental offices, scholarly reports or speeches. In fact, the only group that is given blame but not given the opportunity to be heard is the hip-hop culture that students are embedded in. This occurs despite the fact that hip-hop continually weighs in on the issues surrounding the effectiveness of school. Unfortunately, this voice is not acknowledged in dominant discourse.

In essence, the inadequacies of teachers and the performance of students may simply reflect the inability for those in education to fully understand the culture of students. Therefore, I argue that the deficiencies of urban education and urban science education in particular are reflective of the inability of different groups to fulfil their roles as they relate to the needs of urban youth. For example, an institution committed to urban education that does not have a class in either urban or multicultural education reflects an unwillingness of the institution to take responsibility for effectively preparing pre-service teachers for teaching students who identify themselves as hip-hop. Furthermore, when these classes do exist, the absence of conversations about the nuances of urban youth culture, and conversations about hip-hop and the cursory overview of the existence of non-dominant communities and cultures that omits hip-hop are problematic. Even governmental policies and their offshoots (like standardized exams) that are proposed to improve urban education oftentimes function only to alienate students through their lack of relevance to student culture. In the disingenuous search for equity and accountability, all we have found is more people to blame for our collective inadequacies in meeting the needs of urban youth.

Through my interrogation of urban science education, and the many groups of people who have been blamed for its struggles, the focus on who is to blame for the poor academic achievement within urban schools has been perpetual. This focus on who is to blame often leads to discussions about the extent of dysfunction in urban youth's lives and the role of hip-hop in this dysfunction. In response, I argue that what is dysfunctional to some, makes perfect sense for others. Therefore, blaming the dysfunction within a group for their underperformance in schools without looking at the functionality within the group is more of an effort in placing blame for the sake of maintaining a problem rather than for the sake of finding a solution.

In the case of hip-hop, if it did not exist, enumerable permutations of who is to blame for the poor outcomes in urban areas would remain a major discussion in urban education that needed to be addressed. However, sicne it does exist, and it is the culture of urban youth, it is easier to blame it for many issues that plague urban education.Therefore, I argue that institutions that function on a more macro scale such as boards of education or teacher education programs, and groups that function on a more meso and micro scale who have direct access to urban youth, are equally to blame for not fully enacting their ability to implement direct change that can positively affect instruction in classrooms (Kennedy & Kennedy, 1996, Kincheloe, 1991).

As the issues surrounding urban science education surmount, and schools produce scientists at a lower and lower rate, we have a situation where science education in the country is in danger (UNESCO, 2004). As Douglas (1994) suggests, "it may be a general trait of human society that fear of danger tends to strengthen the lines of division in a community" (p. 34). This is particularly the case because "the poor who carry the brunt are usually to blame for epidemic disaster (p.34)." In the case of urban science education, somewhere between the general discussions on who is to blame, and the scholarly work that presents certain groups as wholly responsible for the issues that plague urban science classrooms, none of the groups discussed above are completely to blame for these situations. However, with no one in particular to blame, all are responsible.

POWER TO TEACH SCIENCE = POWER TO CONTROL: AT THE ROOT OF THE BLAME GAME

I believe that blame is usually a mask for one's inadequacies, or when it is placed on others, a way to mask an unrealistic view of self that forces one to view others as not up to one's own standards. In science education, this is certainly the case. In 1971, Kilpatrick, who was an editor of an issue of the Journal of Science Education questioned why there was a shortage of physical science teachers. He also questioned whether science is truly "dull, alien, introspective, masculine, unintelligible and laborious" (Kilpatrick, 1971) or if it is just presented as such. In an opening essay, he concluded that a possible reason for why science may be viewed negatively is the need for scientists and science educators to assert that they are of "a special breed" that alone possess the ability to understand science. He then discussed an inclination found in those who teach science to feel it is their duty to look for students who have the "honor" to be "disciplined in that hard, cruel, introspective, alien society" known as science.

The clarity and accuracy of the argument made by Kilpatrick has proven to be timeless. It persists in contemporary science education and causes those who teach science to believe they guard the turf reserved for scientists from those who cannot withstand the rigors of the discipline. This belief alienates those who are a part of a culture that is perceived as not disciplined enough to partake in academic challenges like the "hard sciences" and causes a blaming of those who are not perceived as able to achieve for having challenges in achieving. I have witnessed this guarding of the turf of science against intruders play out in contemporary urban science classrooms with new science teachers (in the field for 3 years or less) who hold undergraduate degrees in the sciences.

In my research with these teachers, I find that they enter science teaching with the ideology that their college degrees are the ammunition that they need for taking on a war on science illiteracy or non-achievement in urban students. They have confidence in their "scientific knowledge" and college degrees and believe that science teaching is the process through which they can or should convert the confidence they hold in their science backgrounds into some sort of power to teach. Unfortunately, their unbridled enthusiasm and belief in their power to teach science is often expressed in a way that becomes a power that alienates hip-hop youth from science.

My use of the words ammunition and war in the paragraph above come from my attempt to reflect the ideologies that many science teachers in urban settings hold. These perspectives are derived from my conversations with teachers who have described scenarios in urban science classrooms where they have encountered students that they felt they could not reach. The use of these words (ammunition and war) by teachers projects a belief that interacting with an urban student requires the teacher to possess both the ability to show brute force in teaching and knowledge about science. This notion has permeated the fabric of teacher preparation programs and has become imprinted into the approach to pedagogy of science teachers who enter into urban classrooms under the false assumption that they are prepared to teach science. The reality is that familiarity or even expertise with a specific science content area is never enough preparation for teaching in any setting. Furthermore, within urban settings, where the culture of the student and that of the teacher are often at odds (because of the socioeconomic, race, age, and gender divides that often exist between students who are a part of hip-hop and teachers), the probability of teachers having experiences that vary from those of their students is high. In these instances, the illusion that one holds a power to teach because of a degree in science or a power over the participant in hip-hop because she is a science teacher or scientist will only result in the students' unwillingness to have any type of communication with the teacher and the perpetuation of existent divides between students and science.

During my research, when I have asked the newly minted science teachers to describe the urban students that they teach or will be teaching, each of the characteristics that they described was a picture of a specific media generated hip-hop persona or characteristic. The teachers often discussed the students' baggy attire, the way they speak, the way they walk, and even the type of music they listen to, and did so in very negative ways. As they made these descriptions, they rarely connected the fact that they were working in urban settings with the fact that they were teaching students who are hip-hop or that their descriptors of urban youth were synonymous with the student's hip-hop identity. Consequently, I have concluded that these teachers' descriptions were either unintentionally superficial, coming from a deficit lens with which they viewed hip-hop culture, or indicated that the teachers were only at the beginning point of truly understanding urban students and their distinct culture.

As I curiously engaged in further conversations with these teachers, it also became evident that they believed that the process of effectively teaching, which they saw as having the power to teach and control, involved being able to eliminate the presence of attributes that they saw as markers/descriptors of traditional urban students and hip-hop; such as speaking loudly or with conviction, talking out of turn (which oftentimes meant finishing each other's sentences), or being too "excited." In other words, for these teachers, teaching science meant that the teacher should be able to wield her power to the extent that she could erase the students' ability to interact in ways that they would in social fields outside of the classroom where they were expressing their hip-hop culture.

In the urban classroom, the power to teach that teachers wield comes face to face with the power that urban students hold as a participant in hip-hop. Power in this context refers to one of the many offshoots of one's culture and the entitlement one has that allows her to act. Therefore, the student's power is theoretically similar to that of the teacher. The students' power, like that of their teachers, comes from their experiences, their ways of looking at the world, and their practices. It is what they feel entitled to because of their experiences. Teachers feels like they have the power to teach because of their education and the science knowledge they have, while students feel like they have power because of their ability to survive the everyday challenges of living in urban settings. While the structure of how power is constructed here is similar with students and teachers, the main point to focus on in regards to the power of the student and that of the teacher is how they are expressed in the urban science classroom, and the ways they either support or hinder the connection of hip-hop participants to science.

Power to Teach and Power to Learn

The mass of information, facts, skills and abilities that make up one's culture (schema and practices) are held in a symbolic toolkit that is drawn upon when an individual feels the information within this toolkit is needed for dealing with a particular situation within a social field (DiMaggio, 1997; Swidler, 1986). The information in this symbolic toolkit gives rise to the power or agency people feel they can enact within a particular field. In other words, the teachers' experiences, feelings about hip-hop, and content knowledge come together and shape their cultural toolkit and what they feel they know about teaching in an urban school. This knowledge (what people feel they know) is valued and validated by the teacher's college diploma or teaching certificate and becomes the teacher's power to teach. Teachers are recognized by society as possessing some type of knowledge and believe that they have this knowledge. Therefore, they believe they have the power to teach.

For hip-hop students, the experiences of living in a complex world riddled with obstacles, triumphs, trials and failures causes them to develop an expert knowledge on ways to communicate and navigate within fields outside of the classroom where hip-hop culture is enacted. Just as the teacher holds the college degree as a marker of successes, students in urban schools hold on to hip-hop as evidence of their expertise in being hip-hop. Through their involvement in hip-hop (participation in activities that foster their knowledge of, and participation in the culture), urban youth develop the ability to hold themselves in esteem within any scenario they find themselves. In certain places they feel like they can express the power that comes with the hip-hop knowledge they have. However where they feel silenced or challenged, they feel like they are not empowered.

The ability to express one's power when challenged or silenced is an integral part of the hip-hop cultural toolkit and is part of "humans' amazing ability to store vast stocks of knowledge and to retrieve this knowledge for use in a particular encounter" (Turner, 2002). The ability of human beings to retrieve the knowledge they possess, and enact it in certain ways based on the contexts where they find themselves, plays out vividly in classrooms with both students and teachers. In the classroom where a teacher expresses her power to teach as a power to control or silence the student and the student's culture, students enact their power or agency in different ways. This may range from choosing not to interact with the teacher, to choosing to engage in a power struggle with the teacher. In the latter case, the process of exhibiting her power when one is challenged goes beyond the effect of a controlling teacher in the classroom. For example, when students who are a part of hip-hop are engaged in a rap battle (where they compete with each other to see who is the better emcee), the clash of power that occurs in the battle emerges into a more heightened level of exchange. In this hip-hop field, the exhibition of hip-hopness is glowingly apparent in the visceral responses they have during the exchange within a battle. At its height, a demonstration of the best of the lyrical ability of each of the battle's participants is accompanied by the display of a feeling of superiority over the person that is being battled with. This feeling allows the participant in the battle to view their opponents as beneath them and is the key to the reasons why participants in hip-hop develop such unique styles and flamboyant personalities even in the face of adversity or critique. This superiority complex is evident in rap music and is often criticized and misunderstood as braggadocio when artists boast about material things that they own or special abilities that they have.

In the classroom, students express this superiority complex as an air of non-chalance when the teacher is challenging them, or when they feel they are being spoken to in a way that they perceive as threatening. At times, students immersed in hip-hop exhibit behaviors that are intended to give teachers the feeling that they (the students) are above any of the trivial happenings in the classroom and any of the tasks that the teacher has set out. In fact, a number of popular rap songs describe the knowledge developed outside of what is learned in schools as deeper, more rigorous, and more enlightening than whatever is taught in schools.

In the instances when a student tries to get past the superficial nature of dialogue in the classroom, a refusal to do the work that a teacher asks ensues. This unwillingness to do the work may then be confused by the teacher as an inability to do the work. This is what I term the rap battle response to the classroom or the teacher. In order for teachers to engage with students, they have to transform the nature of the classroom exchange from a rap battle to a rap cypher. In these social fields (the cypher), rather than compete to be the better rapper, people work together to share raps and commend each other for their contributions to the current social space they co-inhabit.

Interrogating Power Dynamics: Hip-hop and the Teacher

In laying out issues surrounding the nature and scope of teaching and learning within the contemporary urban science classroom, particularly as they relate to issues of power and knowledge production for teachers and participants in hip-hop, it is necessary to discuss particular fields where the clashes between the power of the student and that of the teacher are heatedly debated. These are spaces where the words and actions of participants in the discussions reflect a deep seeded animosity between two forces, and the residual effects of a power clash between two populations.

In certain spaces produced by rap, the listener is confronted with statements like "F— a school lecture, them lies make me vexed[er]" (Nas, 1994) or "This school s— is a joke" (Dead Prez, 2000). In the places where these lyrics are born, and where they are heard, the words describe such strong negative emotions about schools that the fact that they are laden with obscenities only serves to fully evoke the emotions of the authors in their listeners.

In other fields such as the teachers' lounge, statements like "be mean, be aggressive, because that's the only way to teach these kids" or "these kids are not serious about their education," evoke just as much negative emotional energy as the words of the rap artists quoted above. In these spaces, divides between teachers and urban youth and the angst that they have developed for one another are just as pronounced as they are in some rap lyrics. Through a focus on rap lyrics that speak negatively about school, and the conversations in teachers lounges that speak negatively about urban youth, it is apparent that the power clashes that are seen in schools are rooted in negative emotions that one group has for the other that are, expressed and reinforced both within and outside of the classroom.

In the case of the rap artists, the institutions that their negative emotions are directed towards are not just schools. Any institution that represents an epistemology that places power into the hands of some and attempts to remove it from their hands is where their anger is directed. In fact, in the Dead Prez song mentioned above, the statement is made that "the same people who control the school system, control the whole prison system and the whole social system." This lyric (and others like it), express the fact that for certain populations, the prison system is seen as an extension of the school just as the descriptions of "these kids" by teachers in urban schools reflects not just the students in a particular classroom but all the students who look, dress or act a certain way. The issue here is whether the power that each of these factions possesses and the animosity that the teachers and the hip-hop students have for each other can be resolved so that links between them can be developed.

These links are challenging to develop because the spaces for discussions that focus on the commonalities between teachers and urban students are rarely created. In addition, for both teachers and students, the value of the power of the other is difficult to accept. This is the case because the validation of the power that another party holds is often misread as a giving up of the power one possesses. For example, if a teacher accepts the fact that a student in the classroom has the ability to get the attention of all her peers in the classroom when the teacher doesn't, the teacher believes that the student's power means a loss of her own.

Therefore, while schools validate the knowledge that the science teacher, and the power that the college degree provides this teacher, that same knowledge is believed to be "lies" and "a joke" to the hip-hop participant. To participants in hip-hop, the knowledge the teacher possesses does not align with, support, or even recognize the power that students have. Conversely, the belief that hip-hop contains information that is based on valuable knowledge that its participants possess is absent among teachers. What the student knows is that teachers do not see hip-hop as conveying any valuable information. This lack of value for each other's culture is a recurrent theme in rap music and in urban education and is exacerbated when youth who are a part of hip-hop are forced to conform to the confines of school systems whose ideological goals do not focus or place value on these students' strengths.

THE POSITIVISTS VERSUS THE LYRICISTS

Kincheloe (2001) discusses the positivist argument, which says that all knowledge, if it is real knowledge, is scientific and is therefore empirically verifiable. In so doing, he lays the framework for one of the key issues why teachers with a degree in the sciences believe that they have a sufficient amount of knowledge and power to teach science. He lays out the fact that among teachers there is an understanding that the knowledge they possess is verifiable by their possession of a degree in science. Conversely, they believe that knowledges like that of hip-hop participants are not valued because they are not verifiable. To compound this issue, the belief that teaching science is a profession that requires specific skills or abilities conjoins with a belief that participation in hip-hop merely involves talking or rhyming and not a sophisticated understanding. Therefore, the general conceptualization of teaching science in urban schools is that the teachers' responsibility is to utilize their special skills to teach something that is "empirically verifiable" and dismiss everything else.

Unfortunately, this ontology has been adopted by many teacher education programs that condense the art of teaching science into a distinct set of pre-described under-standings that if possessed can be the marker of a good teacher and produce science knowledge among urban youth. In so doing (adopting this ontology), the "uncertainty of professional practice was (is) scientifically eliminated and replaced with verifiable empirical knowledge about the art of teaching" (Kincheloe, 2001, p. 79). Consequently, the expectation is that any teacher with a science background who understands the curriculum that she will teach during an academic year is prepared for all possible scenarios in the classroom, will have all the right answers for all scientific inquiries, and will be able to address any possible situations that will occur in the classroom. There is a belief that there is a finite amount of possible scenarios or teaching moments that can occur in the classroom. The well-prepared and skilful science teacher is believed to have the appropriate response to all of these scenarios. In this type of classroom, students who are from a culture like hip-hop (that is based on an ever-evolving social climate with varying forms of communication and an inherent appreciation for improvisation), provide a challenge for a teacher, and school system that is expecting everything within the classroom to fit into the hyper-structured mold that is created.

This approach to teaching where there is an answer for every possible scenario that occurs in the classroom, coupled with the belief that a prescribed curriculum and sufficient science content knowledge can make a good science teacher are the ingredients for an ineffective science classroom. A teacher that comes to the classroom only with the tools mentioned above cannot effectively communicate with students, especially those posited in a culture where the only consistency in their communication rests in its multi-phonic and improvisational nature.

In the urban classroom, where the power of the teacher is expressed in the ability to constrain thoughts and actions that extend beyond a prescribed curriculum, the practices of the effective science teacher revolve around mundane and basic points that have nothing to do with delivering instruction. Teaching becomes relegated to the ability to keep students in their seats, give them a specific amount of information and ensure that they relay that same information back to the teacher in an assessment. This kind of structure results in the alienation of students who are hip-hop participants from science and an increase in the probability that power clashes between students and the teacher will occur. This situation turns every exchange between the student and teacher into a situation where a rap battle response is ready to be activated. In these situations, words are being spouted but no true exchange occurs and the gulf between students and teachers is expanded.

Learning From Hip-hop and Rap: Understanding Misconceptions

The struggle of certain students to engage with science in more corporate science classrooms occurs because in hip-hop, everything from dance, art, and rap (which even when it is confined to the generic 5 minute, verse and chorus formula of popular music), contains prolific improvisation that expresses the shared connection of participants in the culture to each other and to hip-hop. When participants in the culture who are from a lower socioeconomic status have to deal with issues like not knowing where their next meal is coming from, or not having a safe venue to meet with peers after school, the ability to create solutions to problems as they unfold, and work together to attack a shared problem is treasured. In one of my research projects in a chemistry laboratory and classroom, the students would rush through the specific steps of a chemistry lab because they would be able to conduct their own mini experiments when the assigned lab was over. When the assigned lab tasks were complete, they would gather around in a group that mimicked a rap cypher and conduct their own experiments with the materials from the classroom lab. The students would pose questions to each other, present possible answers to the questions posed, and perform experiments to prove and disprove each other's questions. These same students would nod in unison while counting the number of drops being placed into a beaker as though they were nodding to a rap song. They would collectively sigh when the results of their experiments produced expected results and cheer when they thought they were embarking on something new.

Within the structure of the conventional chemistry classroom, with an established state curriculum and state approved pacing calendar, these same students would sit silently, refuse to answer questions and fail to interact with the teacher. They would talk to the teacher in ways that were almost opposite to the ways that they interacted in the laboratory - when they had the opportunity to truly engage in science that was authentic for them. In these types of scenarios, the scientifically verifiable teaching practice that occurred in the chemistry classroom alienated students who otherwise would engage in science when more appropriate structures were in place to facilitate their freedom to discover on their own.

In another science classroom, the teacher would often interrupt the lesson to step into the hallway. In further conversations with him about this practice, he mentioned that when he heard students speaking loudly in the hallway, he thought that they were about to get into a fight and so, he went into the hallway to stop them from fighting. In addition, whenever this teacher felt uncomfortable with the level of noise or the hand gestures that students used when they were having discussions in the classroom, he would assume that their conversations would lead to a more heated argument. In response, he would stop his lesson to try to calm students down and either call security or another teacher. As the teacher tried to control the classroom behavior, the class sat and waited for whatever scenario the teacher saw as potentially problematic to play out even though valuable class time was being wasted.

In dialogues with students and the teacher about the fact that students could not always get through an entire lesson, the teacher complained about the students' behavior and argued that their tendency to be loud and/or "violent" was the cause of the wasted time. Through further conversations, the students were able to let the teacher know that his exaggerated responses to student discussions and his assumption that students were going to fight were unwarranted because the discussions that they were having would never go beyond a verbal exchange. The students mentioned that in almost every scenario where the teacher expected that a fight was going to happen, they were merely talking, playing, and ready to learn if they were prompted to do so.

With an awareness of the nature of heated exchanges which are seen in hip-hop through rap battles, and a familiarity with the fact that artists speak loudly to each other just to acknowledge each other and hold a conversation, the understanding would be in place that when participants in hip-hop are emotionally invested in making a point to a peer, modes of exchange that vary from what the teacher considers normal may be expressed. However, those who are outside of hip-hop, as a result of their invalidation of the culture, do not understand that these types of exchanges are not precursors to violent behavior. In fact, the students' position as a part of hip-hop necessitates an emotional and visceral response in a verbal exchange. In other words, what is common knowledge to hip-hop is a cause for alarm and an opportunity to cast the participants in hip-hop into a negative light by those outside of the culture.

Beyond its anecdotal value, the scenarios within the chemistry classroom described above outline the implications of misunderstanding aspects of hip-hop culture. They also provide much evidence for a couple of major issues related to schools and hip-hop and hip-hop and science teaching. Firstly, they demonstrate the extent of misconceptions about students that perpetuate the students' frustration with the structures of the science classroom. Secondly, they outline the importance of having dialogues with students, and lastly, they underscore the importance of understanding the modes of communication in hip-hop and how they may become productively incorporated in the classroom.

Addressing Basic Misconceptions about Hip-hop Students

As mentioned earlier, urban students' frustrations within classrooms come from preconceived notions that educators (and sometimes researchers) hold about students who are hip-hop. While I have discussed blatant misconceptions like the hip-hop students' disinterest in education or their inability to be successful academically, one of the most pervasive misconceptions that have a direct implication on urban science education is that urban students who are hip-hop are violent. In many instances, this belief in hip-hop's propensity for violence results in the removal of materials for teaching science or engaging in science such as glass, sharp objects, or even meter sticks. This misconception usually comes from images of hip-hop in the media that highlight shootings and stabbings, and instill fear in those who are outside of urban communities. This fear gets transferred into schools throughout urban areas, and the fear of students inflicting harm on each other or teachers ends up being a reason for denying them access to materials that they need to actively engage in science. Interviews with students have shown that in some instances, students are asked to skip certain assignments in a statewide curriculum because of the fact that the materials in a specific lab activity are perceived to be too dangerous for them to handle. Meanwhile, students in other settings who are not viewed as part of hip-hop are allowed to engage in these activities and use tools such as scalpels or glassware without issue.

Another prevalent misconception is that participants in hip-hop are unapproachable or unwilling to discuss their educational needs and concerns. This misconception is one that is consistently debunked by students with whom I conduct research. When asked to engage in conversations about their educational experiences in and outside of classrooms with teachers and researchers, they give tremendous time and effort to ensure that their thoughts and opinions about the science classroom are discussed. In fact, while the students were almost always readily willing to engage in these discussions, initial attempts to get teachers to engage in discussions with students revealed that they were less willing to do so.

I argue that it is important to develop a unique understanding of the misconceptions that exist and look at the role they play in the automatic positioning of students as criminal and other than academically inclined. When one can go beyond these misconceptions and develop more deep understandings of students' lifeworlds, they reveal a profound interest in being successful in social fields such as science classrooms. Furthermore, I argue that the positioning of students' knowledge as outside of societal norms through the use of codes that are based on misconceptions is problematic. The use of terms like "appropriate behavior" or "well behaved" as a marker of how a student should act in schools is an understated yet rampant practice implemented by many urban schools that affects the ways students are treated in classrooms. While these terms are supposed to provide comments on how a child is doing, or chart the students' academic progress, they function to maintain deficit perspectives about hip-hop youth and prevent their full participation in the intellectual life of the classroom. This is the case because their exhibition of hip-hopness is usually classified as inappropriate or seen as poor behavior. When this incessant disregard for the students hip-hopness is perpetuated, it only results in the production of a more hard-hitting denouncing of schools in avenues like rap music where students can define who they are without being pre-judged.

USING RAP TO UNDERSTAND MISCONCEPTIONS: REFOCUSSING MISCONCEPTIONS OF URBAN YOUTH

In my experiences as a secondary school physics and chemistry teacher, I often found that the students who exhibited the most resistance to school were often the ones most entrenched in hip-hop. These were the students who wanted to be rappers, were part of rap groups, were dancers, poets, graffiti artists or beat boxers. I also realized that once these students were presented with the fact that their stance as participants in hip-hop did not mean that they were outside of what is appropriate or normal in school, and once I allowed them to understand that their being a part of hip-hop was not separate from success in science, their level of achievement in science classes tremendously increased. These students began to understand that their participation in hip-hop provided them with more insight and a deeper understanding of science than their peers in other settings. They also performed well on markers like classroom participation, science based projects, standardized exams, and classroom tests. In some instances, they began to speak about science concepts with ease and expressed their scientific knowledge in more complex ways than I ever expected them to (Emdin, 2008). In essence, the societal perception and labelling of hip-hop students as uncivil, unruly and unmanageable causes them to be taught by teachers as though they in fact embody these qualities. This, in turn, causes them to exhibit the qualities that they are expected to enact. In instances where these negative expectations do not exist, or when students are ensured that being who they are does not mean that they have to be unsuccessful in school, they strive to become successful and then do so.

An example of the behaviors that students exhibit when negative perceptions and low expectations are pushed upon them is described in the song "Nobody Knows" by rapper Nelly (2005). In this song, he describes being "through eight different schools in twelve different years, about thirty different teachers, over ten thousand different peers." In the song, he also discusses how he fought in school and was repetitively suspended. As I listened to this lyric, I was struck by the similarities of the rapper's experience to that of a young man who was suspended from his former school and sent to the high school where I taught. I remember his hip-hop persona/swagger, and the tough exterior that he came into the class with, and how the wall he had put up to shield himself from showing any emotion dissipated the very instant that he was validated when he showed the most remote interest in a classroom discussion that related the concept of motion to riding the subway.

During the lesson, he was given an opportunity to express his knowledge about the subway system and compared the motion of a moving train to Newton's laws of motion. When the realization was made that I did not equate his being suspended from his former school or the fact that he was wearing a bandana that represented a gang stand as a reason why he should be silenced in class, he consistently engaged in the class. Under normal circumstances, the scenario that would occur with a student who seemed to be other than school or science is described by Rapper Rhymefest in a lyric that says "I'm born in the ghetto, I'm a product of society, I blame my eighth grade teacher for trying to silence me, yeah I act violently" (Rhymefest, 2007). In other words, inappropriate or even violent action or behavior often stems from the absence of an opportunity to have voice or to actively communicate within the structures of the classroom. In order to provide voice and foster students' active communication in the science classroom, a new approach to science pedagogy that targets those who have traditionally been silenced by working towards actively involving them in the classroom is necessary.

The teaching and research approach that I call for, which involves a process of learning and or utilizing the complex nuances of communication in hip-hop is far removed from the scientifically verifiable approach to pedagogy that is currently in place. It requires a process where constant exchange with students is necessary and conclusions about what is working in the classroom are consistently formed and reformed. This process is more complex than the traditional approach to pedagogy because of the fact that it involves an ongoing process where the teacher continually learns more about how to teach from hip-hop (the culture and its people) and continually adds new information to what Swidler (1986) refers to as the cultural toolkit. This toolkit simply serves as a space where the information one receives is stored and then drawn upon when necessary. Continually adding to one's cultural toolkit allows for a redefinition of one's preconceived notions with the addition of information that either challenges or adds to what one believes. Through an awareness of one's misunderstandings of hip-hop, and an active search to learn more about the culture, one may combat pre-existent notions or thoughts about it. In this process, the teacher begins to see the power struggles that exist between self and the hip-hop student as a struggle between past knowledges about the hip-hop student and new experiences as a learner of hip-hop. The act of teaching becomes a way to not only disseminate information but also increase an under-standing of hip-hop. This complex, yet valuable, process fails to garner much recognition within traditional urban science classrooms because "the higher our levels of epistemological understanding, the weaker our perspectives often appear to a culture that has been conditioned to buy into a quest for certainty" (Kincheloe, 1999, p. 287). The teacher who focuses her science instruction on hip-hop and the students' understandings of that culture may be perceived as too non-traditional and hence not a good teacher. This is particularly the case if the class becomes louder than others (even if it is a result of increased participation) or where the traditional structure of the science classroom (sitting quietly and being docile) is absent.

NATURE OF HIP HOP AND SCIENCE TEACHING: IN TRUTH AND FABRICATION

Arendt (1958), in her articulation of the processes that we need for existence, and the activities we embark upon within the world, discusses the nature of phenomena that take root in thought through art and poetry. She also mentions that these phenomena are the closest things to living recollection and pure thought. Hip-hop, which is a culture that is rooted in the merging of the thoughts of the marginalized as they are expressed through art and poetry, serves as a brilliant example of how such phenomena can become the manifestation of all the thoughts, experiences, feelings and emotions of a certain population. Arendt then goes on to mention how "...the lovers of results in the sciences have never tired of pointing out how entirely useless thought is" (Arendt, 1958, p. 170). Through her work, the variance between hip-hop and science is clearly pronounced and the implications of the differences between these two domains on urban science education are made available to the teacher and researcher.

In the traditional science classroom, teachers function as the "lovers of results in the sciences" that Arendt describes and teach without an explicit focus on developing or validating thought which lies outside of the realm of science or the curriculum. Rather than teach to foster new thought, science teaching and learning becomes a process that I term cognition within parameters. In other words, instruction is nested in a focus on cognition as long as it fosters reasoning, perceiving, or inducing to meet an already determined and specified result. Hip-hop's artistic and poetic quality, and its ability to reify and quantify new thoughts and feelings into art and poetry through rhythm and rhyme, stands in opposition to the conventional approach to science teaching, which consists of delivering prescribed information to students in classrooms without giving them an opportunity to fully process or question the phenomena presented to them. Despite this variance from science, hip-hop finds a way to realign itself to the discipline in the sense that it focuses on inquiry, discovery, making meaning, and then sharing one's thoughts.

Hip-hop, through rap, is a culture founded on implementing and developing new thought and the transformation of these thoughts into realms beyond existent parameters. The "poets means to achieve [the] transformation is rhythm" (Arendt, 1958 p. 169) and hip-hop is rooted in rhythm. This rhythm is evident in the way that participants in the culture walk and talk in their communities or in the beats that are the backdrop to the raps formed by hip-hop participants. I argue that this same rhythm can also be evident in science classrooms where rhythm and synchrony have become a marker that signifies when students engaged in hip-hop are fully engaged in the classroom. I find that the seamlessness with which a teacher and students exchange turns at talk, the consistency in the pauses between talk, and the similarity of their head nods during discourse in science classrooms, indicate a certain rhythm that is absent when students are not engaged in the classroom.

Where There is More Than Meets the Eye: Let the Rhythm Hit 'Em'

In my graduate work as a cell biology researcher, one of the first tasks that I was responsible for was the creation of agarose gels for electrophoresis. Despite the fact that I was taught how to create the gels, and constantly went over the steps I was taught in my head, I often nervously fumbled through the process and would rarely finish my assigned task. When my frustration with this process became evident, the expert researcher in the lab would often mention that the gels sensed my nervousness and fear and that controlling my emotions and my feelings of being brand new in the lab would rectify the issues I was having. What I was being told was that my negative emotions about the process of creating the gels affected the activity I was engaged in. After some time, I was able to overcome my negative emotions. Once this happened, I was able to succeed at my tasks.

My discovery that taking stock of my emotions had an effect on my ability to complete a task in the lab caused me to begin paying attention to the role of emotions in the completion of science tasks in the lab. I noticed that the scientists would often describe the results of experiments or processes that we engaged in as beautiful. At times, the lead researcher would mention that putting the speed on the centrifuge too high would upset the cells. There would be music playing in the background during experiments and a constant search for positive emotions among all researchers and students who worked in the laboratory. These instances serve as examples of how "hard" science research moves beyond the traditional mechanistic and positivistic model despite the fact that it presents itself as completely rigid in the classroom. My experiences in the laboratory proved that anytime that we interact with an object or person; we come to create a new layer of multi-logicality that provides opportunities for richness in future work. Each interaction with the scientists and materials in the lab was so laden with emotion that the quest for knowledge merged with positive emotions like happiness and excitement to define what science should be.

In science education, the need for teachers or researchers to follow the positivistic approach to instruction that they believe is the approach used by scientists causes them to follow an archaic model that is pursued at the expense of embracing an emotional dimension, which is more intuitive and often more effective for true learning to occur. Richness, as referred to in the previous paragraph requires comfort with a socio-emotional approach to the work that may be ambiguous or different from familiar notions of traditional schooling and science. Embracing richness in the teaching process translates into an openness to the effects of hip-hop on the teaching and learning process because it generates the same kinds of positive emotions that are seen in the science lab.

In a rich and descriptive approach to the work, the search for positive emotions also includes an active search for pictures of what the fields that hip-hop participants inhabit look like from their perspective. For example, in my work, students' vivid descriptions of the high-rise project buildings they live in, lead to how these pictures either vary from, or are similar to, the ways that the teacher or researcher views the same fields, these conversations then become the fodder for classroom discussions about how these pictures relate to science. In my work, I consistently look for opportunities for students to tap into this aesthetic dimension because I believe that it is essential to understanding the ways that students make sense of the classroom.

In hip-hop, vivid descriptions are commonplace and are a part of each of the major components of the culture. In graffiti, dance and rap, the artistry is embedded in providing descriptions of the artist's experiences. In each of these artifacts, the artist tells a tale either through voice, movement or picture and through her art, provides descriptions of the neighborhood, the school, or the teacher. The student who is immersed in hip-hop is also an artist, and can provide everything from a collage of beautiful pictures about the classroom fields that the teacher perceives as challenging/troubling to a piercing reflection of the dysfunction within a class that the teacher may feel is a normally functioning field.

The pictures that students provide are valuable resources for teachers because of the breadth of information they contain on how the teacher teaches, how the student learns and how hegemony, politics, and semiotics play a role in the way the student perceives the classroom and in making sense of the mindsets of participants in hip-hop.

Teachers and researchers cannot make sense or meaning of hip-hop, and the interactions of participants in hip-hop using the finite and positivistic ways that teachers traditionally deliver a scientific topic. While it is important not to completely dismiss what is considered to be positivistic knowledge because it is a way of knowing (just as the post structuralist epistemology which I am laying out for working with participants in hip-hop is a framework for acknowledging a way of knowing), the objective is to utilize this knowledge as a point from which we delve deeper.

An Approach to Making Meaning of Hip-hop

Rap artist T.I., like many other rap artists, paints pictures of how the urban student interacts with school. In one lyric, he mentions that, "O.G.'s (original gangsters) say a lot of them, they see in me, cuz I'm a scholar, no diploma, no G.E.D." (T.I., 2005). These words provide deep insight into the dynamics at play in the mind of a person who has been marginalized from school, and who despite that fact, has a feeling of superiority over schools. As T.I. describes himself as a scholar despite not having a diploma or passing a high school equivalency exam, he evokes a level of confidence that would not be expected from a person who has not been successful in formal education.

While this confidence may not make much sense to someone who is outside of hip-hop, a phenomenological approach to making sense of this lyric is necessary. This approach, which requires putting oneself in the shoes of another person, and in this case, becoming the participant in hip-hop who crafted the lyric, allows the listener to more effectively understand where the rapper is coming from. The person who takes the lens of T.I. may begin by searching for answers to what it means to be a scholar with no diploma or G.E.D. By seeking to understand what it feels like to be in this position, the search for answers to questions about the possible experiences within schools that lead the rapper to making his statements about being a scholar becomes a personal quest for the listener. This approach also allows the listener to temporarily hold the power that the author of the lyric has, and understand what the indirect message to schooling that his lyric provides is. Through this journey, the student of hip-hop culture, who may be the teacher or researcher, gains insight into hip-hop's general perceptions of school and schooling and has the opportunity to hold these new perspectives against the perceptions held before these phenomena were being looked at through the lens of a participant in hip-hop.

Understanding the experiences that gave birth to a lyric, or engaging in a process that looks to understand these phenomena by attempting to answer the questions one may have had about hip-hop, and then working towards experiencing it through a phenomenological approach to an artist's life through his lyrics, provides new definitions and understandings and provides the science educator with a new paradigm to investigate when teaching science.

By working to understand the meaning of T.I.'s lyric, I was led to a conversation with a student about the notion of the O.G. While I had always known what the term meant, I discovered that the O.G. is celebrated in contemporary hip-hop because to be an O.G. (original gangster) is to have been able to successfully navigate through the travails of life as a participant in hip-hop and still be able to retain one's "streetness" or ability to relate to or understand the streets. In hip-hop, there is a concept called "having a hood pass" that permits a person or people who has left the streets by getting a college education, or having money, to return to the streets. The hood pass is also extended to someone who is not from the "streets" but who is accepted as a part of the community. The hood pass allows those who have been granted one to retain the privileges afforded to participants in hip-hop even though they may not remain in the same physical place or neighborhood. This pass is extended to people who exhibit characteristics that allow a core hip-hop audience to relate to them because their words and actions are true to the culture. A White female teacher from suburbia who teaches in an urban school may be extended a hood pass because of her ability to express her biases and misconceptions about urban students while working towards teaching phenomenologically and exhibiting a willingness to understand hip-hop and teach science in ways that relate to the students' experiences.

The converse to the granting of a hood pass to someone who is not born into hip-hop is the revoking of a hood pass for someone who at some point was hip-hop. The fact that success within school settings is often implemented in ways that force students to be stripped of their hip-hop persona (even if they are not learning), often leads to the proliferation of the notion that going through school successfully equates to a feeling that "they (schools) done stole your streetness" (West, 2007) and becomes a part of the normal discourse in hip-hop. This streetness is one's connection to the hip-hop community and is the most valued and treasured attribute of someone who has had experiences outside of traditional hip-hop circles that has managed to maintain their connection to the culture. In the perfect scenario, science instruction in urban schools would constitute an incorporation of students' identities and hip-hop culture in conjunction with more traditional ways of knowing so that streetness or hiphopness does not have to be separate from school.

The fact that methods of instruction in urban science classrooms favor students who sit quietly and who have no true involvement in science and little to no opportunities to engage in inquiry about the discipline but have no "behavior problems" has caused many science teachers to believe that this pedagogical approach is what urban science teaching is. This causes teachers to view students who attempt to move towards actual science by asking questions that are not part of the script of the curriculum as disruptive or enacting a hip-hop persona that challenges their instruction. The fact that this identification of the persona of the hip-hop student with non-achievement or with negative connotations even when it is actually tied to inquiry and discovery (which are integral to true participation in science) displays the need to embark on a battle to expose the flaws in established ideas about the ways to teach urban youth. Furthermore, it exposes the deficiencies of the current methods of teaching science that fail to connect with hip-hop youth. The absence of a focus on hip-hop and on the hip-hop generation, and the lack of an effort of educators to see the world through the eyes of the participant in hip-hop ignores the impact of the social, political and physical constructs that shape urban students' attitudes towards schools and negatively impacts their ability to connect to science.

Choosing Your Lens

In their vivid descriptions of the spirit of the inner city and the social and economic agents that shape their lives, hip-hop artists describe the experiences that inner city students bring to schools that should force a restructuring of existent perceptions and modes of thought on their instruction in schools. Rapper, Common, describes his experience within what is described as the "inner city" with cold nights, heating a home with a heated stove, and dreaming of freedom from the struggles he experiences in the world. In the same song, he describes his journey into higher education and how it resulted in a "college career that got downed with a couple of beers" (Common, 2005). The artist's descriptions can be viewed in two very distinct ways that can both serve as accurate descriptions of the classic experiences of many Black males in academic institutions. The autobiography he provides could stand as both the story of a person who didn't have what it took to succeed in formal educational institutions or the story of someone that has the ability to articulate his experiences, describe the challenges of it and construct a vivid picture of his experiences within schools. The story that is taken away by the listener is dependent upon the lens that the person listening chooses to take. There can be a more dismissive lens, or a more inclusive one. I argue for a perspective that sees the participant in hip-hop as dissimilar from an established norm but not deficient in comparison to it. With this lens, notions of good and bad students, labels of intelligent, brilliant, science minded, or disinterested that are too often tagged to students are acknowledged to be socially constructed and not truly indicative of anything substantial. With a more inclusive lens, it becomes clear to the educator that believing that certain people do not possess positive attributes because of their embeddedness in a certain culture is a flawed approach to teaching and research that only serves to separate students from science and school.

FROM THE GLOBAL TO THE LOCAL: HIP-HOP, SCIENCE EDUCATION, AND THE RITUAL

A couple of months ago, I had an opportunity to go on a nine-hour drive with my father. We don't get a chance to spend time together very often and I always enjoy the time we share together. Each time we get a chance to talk, the nuggets of wisdom that I am able to take away from our conversations are priceless. The day of this trip, he drove up to the front of my house, honked his car horn and I jumped excitedly into the passenger seat of his car like I did when I was six years old. Just like he did when I was younger, he asked me to put on my seatbelt; he cracked the car window about an inch on each side, and started to play his music. I sank back comfortably in my seat, and for the next few hours listened to the best of the 1970's. Al Green, The Commodores, and Sam Cooke provided a serenade to our ride and I was transported back to my early teens, when I discovered these songs on my own by digging into my father's record collection. About 4 hours into our drive, both of our 6-foot plus frames had grown tired from being folded into the cramped seats of the car. We pulled into a rest stop, stretched our legs a bit and I volunteered to take the wheel.

In my family, the ritual is that whoever drives gets to play the music. So as soon as I got behind the wheel, I plugged in my digital music player. While I had enjoyed my father's music up until this point in our drive, it was my turn to provide the soundtrack to the rest of the ride. As I hit play on the small machine, the intro to Marvin Gaye's Inner City Blues oozed through the speaker. My father smiled as the familiar tune began to play. He loved Marvin Gaye and Inner City Blues was one of his favorite songs. As the intro to the song built to the verse, he looked towards me with a face I cannot describe as Papoose, an underground hip-hop artist began to rap over the music to Marvin Gaye's song. I looked towards my father and smiled as he began to shake his head. We then sat in silence as the rest of the song played. Every few seconds, I would glance at my fathers face in amusement as I tried to read his facial expression as Papoose rapped.

As soon as the song ended, my father looked up at me and said, "Not bad, I liked it." After his initial apprehension about hearing a rap verse being recited over the music to one of his favorite artists, it became clear to him that Papoose had captured the same emotion that Marvin Gaye did. While Marvin Gaye spoke about the feelings of powerlessness that come with being from the "inner city," Papoose talks about the bittersweetness of the inner city experience. On the song, Papoose speaks for, and to participants in hip-hop as he paints pictures of life in the inner city, and how those who are a part of hip-hop move beyond being positioned as victim, and into a space where they are valued and respected for who they are.

The emotion that is evoked from both Marvin Gaye's song Inner City Blues, and Papoose's song Flashbacks, points to one of the most distinctive attributes of hip-hop. It has the ability to transform into a new way of knowing and understanding for populations across generations that are struggling to find voice within urban settings. As it retains this ability to transform, it concurrently maintains the rules and traditions that it stems from and the rituals that make it a distinct culture associated with the marginalized. For example, one can observe socioeconomically disadvantaged youth in Brazil or in New Zealand who listen to and create hip-hop and see that the ways they utilize hip-hop culture is the same as the ways urban youth do in the United States. In these nations, marginalized youth use hip-hop as a tool to express their experiences as the socio-economically disadvantaged or as outsiders to the norm because of their indigenous status. Their gestures, the way they talk, and the ways they interact with each other, show that they embody attributes that are indicative of an immersion in hip-hop culture. Their local cultures merge with hip-hop and then form a new hybridized culture that is often more hip-hop than anything else.

In Nigeria, West Africa, the voice of the oppressed in the 1970s emerged through the music and life of Femi Anikulapo Kuti, whose claim to fame was his self-positioning as the voice of oppressed people in his country. His artistic work was a merging of traditional Yoruba music, funk, jazz and a biting socio-political critique of the powers that be both within, and outside of Nigeria. The captivating rhythms in his work, and the blending of genres that made his music what it is echoes that of hip-hop in its purest form and has been sampled by contemporary hip-hop artists like Common and The Roots. I make this point to highlight the fact that the spirit of hip-hop transcends both time and geographic divides. In a sense, there is no part of the globe where hip-hop culture or its ancestors hasn't reached. This is the case because in every society, there are populations who are denied full participation in an existing social structure. When hip-hop is introduced in these spaces, people who have been oppressed latch on to it and markers of hip-hop within the social spaces they inhabit become pronounced.

These markers of hip-hop are the rituals that the oppressed across the globe engage in. Rituals are one of the chief identifiers of hip-hop, marking it as a distinct culture that is linked to, but is separate from the folk cultures of individuals from different places who have been denied voice. This is why Fela "dubbed his groove AfroBeat because he understood the afro-connections from Black people in Nigeria to Black people in London to Black people he met in his tour of America" (Schoonmaker, 2003, p. 30). Fela understood the magic of music as an avenue for voice just as hip-hop culture has understood the purpose of rap music in continuing in Fela's tradition. Fela, through his hybridized musical style, spoke for Africans across the globe just as the hip-hop scene speaks to the particular struggles of marginalized populations. For him, and for the creators of hip-hop music, there is no variance between the creator and the consumer of the music. The connection that they have to each other is always there, and if it isn't clear, it is identifiable through the shared rituals that they enact.

Ritual here refers to any consistent patterned action that a group of people engage in over a period of time. For example, the ritual that consists of the distinct head nod that participants in a rap cypher enact when they are either rapping or are listening (that will be discussed in more depth later) is the same all over the globe. The ritual of the perfectively timed "yo" or "uh" prior to reciting a rap verse, and the practice of the musician providing a pause when a particularly witty or hard hitting line is recited, are also rituals that participants in hip-hop across the globe have in common that connects them to each other.

In order to grasp more fully what the impact of hip-hop is on the lives of students who are devoted to it, and bring the hip-hop generation into science, it becomes necessary to look closely at the role of ritual in hip-hop. This focus on ritual will contribute to the chief goals of this chapter, which are to provide the reader with more situations where hip-hop has or can inform science classroom teaching and learning, and to discuss the application of the hip-hop ritual in urban science education.

How Crucial is the Ritual?

In my work within classrooms, I view both consistent patterned actions and the responses that they trigger over time as rituals. For example, when a teacher repeatedly makes a certain statement in the class, and then students give a certain reaction to that statement, the statement and the reaction that it evokes, evolve to become rituals. This is particularly the case with students who are a part of hip-hop, whose culture is one that is rooted in ritual. For example, in a chemistry classroom where I conducted research, a teacher returned from a district wide professional development session with a hyper focus on the district curriculum for the rest of that week. In response, the students decided to stop talking to the teacher. Before long, the teacher's practices had become the trigger for the enactment of a student ritual, which was to purposefully not respond to the teacher when she spoke. In another class, the teacher's ritual of yelling to get the students' attention was responded to by students with a ritual of their own, which involved purposefully ignoring the teacher. These two rituals, which are merely examples of many others that I have witnessed in urban science classrooms, stand in distinct contradiction to hip-hop rituals.

As mentioned earlier, when rappers make a noise like "uh" or say the word "yo" three or four times before beginning a rap verse, listeners engage in the ritual of cueing in to the rapper in response. Both the rapper and the listener are engaged in mutually sustaining rituals that function to meet a shared collective goal. Both the ritual that is enacted, and the responses to it, are clearly understood by all participants. Both the rapper and the listener become accustomed to, and prepared for, the activity they are mutually engaged in through the enactment of practices that have evolved to become rituals. As other rituals are enacted in the rap performance, actors within that shared social field co-create other structures that cause the needs of both the rapper and the audience to be met. In this type of scenario, rituals are enacted in order to get an audience's attention and make sure that they are focused on what the rapper is about to say.

My description of the above ritual in hip-hop is not intended to be an argument for science teachers to say "yo" three times to get the students' attention in the classroom (although this may very well be a worthwhile practice) or take a ritual from hip-hop and then try to implement it in the classroom. However, understanding how these rituals are enacted in hip-hop should make the science teacher aware of the fact that if these highly ritualized practices are the key to either engagement or disengagement in hip-hop, they can be the same within the classroom.

The patterned actions that encompass the rituals that either teachers or participants in hip-hop engage in when they are in classroom together serve as a backbone to social interaction among students and teachers. A study of these patterned actions provides insight into how and why certain student behaviors that may not support student success in science are exhibited in the classroom. For example, if a science teacher begins every classroom discussion with a topic/issue that directly relates to his students' neighborhood or daily experience, the teacher's actions develop into a ritual. The positive emotional energy that is generated each time the teacher enacts this ritual results in certain actions from the students that have the potential to grow into other positive rituals. As these student rituals generate positive emotions in the classroom, students enact classroom practices that are conducive to, or supportive of, teaching and learning in the classroom.

Conversely, a lesson that repetitively does not involve students' experiences, or consists of actions that negate their hip-hop identity, results in the generation of negative emotional energy. In response, students express behaviors that reflect this negative emotional state and it becomes more than likely that they begin to enact rituals that show disinterest in the science classroom. McLaren (1986) discusses how the "bland redundancy and oppressive systemacity" of classroom instruction, becomes the ritualized practices of teachers, and the seedbed for "rituals of resistance"(p.80) that students enact in response to oppressive classroom structures. For example, in the midst of a discussion in a classroom I was observing, a teacher mentioned to a student that she should "forget about trying to work on that problem because it was too challenging for you guys (the students in the class) to handle. This statement led to an immediate loud response by the student, and a small argument between the student and teacher. As soon as the rest of the class caught wind of the argument, a situation ensued where all the students came to the defense of their peer. They interpreted the teacher's statement as a perception that the students could not solve challenging problems and from that point on, enacted practices that showed the teacher that they were disinterested in learning from him. In turn, the teacher became defensive and frustrated with the class. Eventually, the norm in the class was a set of rituals where the teacher did not academically challenge the students, and the students were not engaged in the classroom.

Goffman (1997) argues that individuals perform rituals for, and to one another. In the case of students in the urban science classroom, the communal nature of hip-hop, and the students' responsibilities for and to one another, are heightened when they sense a common enemy that threatens one of their own, or their connections to each other. In these types of scenarios, where urban students feel devalued by their teacher, the science class becomes an obstacle that all the students feel like they have to overcome together. Participants in hip-hop overcome this obstacle by not allowing it to control them. In turn, they ignore the teacher, disrupt the lessons being taught, or do whatever is in their power to subvert whatever they believe to be the goal of the teacher or the class. While educators and researchers perceive these behaviors as descriptors of, or markers of, urban students' negative attitudes towards science and school, they are merely reactions to the ostracizing manner in which science content is delivered in the traditional urban classroom.

The abstractness in Hip-hop and Science

Hip-hop is a culture that is based on describing the reality of one's experience as it is taken in by one's senses. This stands in sharp contradiction to the fact that "contemporary science has moved quite far from the historical trust it (once) placed in unaided sense perception" (Wilson, 2003, p. 211). Science has emerged to become a phenomenon used chiefly for explaining things that cannot be seen. In fact, the beauty of many strands of contemporary science is viewed as resting in its abstractness. While I appreciate this element of science, I argue that resting on this abstractness of science inhibits educators from interrogating the tangible pieces of students' immediate worlds. The failure to make this connection to student lifeworlds makes it challenging for youth whose culture focuses on what is real and tangible, to find comfort in science. I argue that school science, in its descriptions of the fundamental tenets of science, fails to recognize the complexity of students' hip-hopness (that includes a description of the students' real life experiences), and the need for its relation to science. In my experiences within urban science class-rooms as a student, my peers and I would always ask how the information being taught relates to our real life. As a teacher and school administrator, I heard this same question being asked by students all the time. When the teacher does not provide an answer to this question when it is posed by students, and continues to talk about science in abstract ways, students who are a part of hip-hop, purposefully and collectively disconnect from the classroom. This disconnection of science to student experience is a process that causes schools, teachers, and science to be recognizable figures that participants in hip-hop can name in their solidarity forming to each other, and in their alienation from schools.

The absence of a real life connection between science and students' lives, fortifies bonds that have already been formed because of the obstacles urban students have overcome outside of the classroom. This bonding together in the face of adversity results in the enactment of additional rituals. These rituals naturally transfer into the classroom through the porous boundaries of social fields. Over time, the process of dealing with structures out of the classroom develops into new rituals that students enact within the classroom. For example, students' responses to gatherings in hip-hop that are broken up by police officers, result in urban youth's forming of close ties to one another and the development of intricate ways of hindering the infiltration of their culture by law enforcement. In response to law enforcements' breaking up of hip-hop gatherings, urban youth develop signals to those who may be breaking the law to alert them of the presence of police, or decide not to give information that may possibly solve a crime.

In the classroom, these out of school rituals get manifested as intentional moves to disrupt the lesson, signalling to peers as to when to disrupt the teacher, or purposefully deciding not to complete assignments. Once these rituals are established, they grow into more nuanced rituals that determine the extent to which students feel either connected to, or disconnected from the classroom. In my research, I find that classrooms that allow for multiple opportunities for the rituals seen in hip-hop like the call and response seen in rap shows and cyphers to become a part of the classroom shos students that their culture is welcome in the class, and generates the same types of positive emotional energy that hip-hop performances do. Statements from the teacher that require a specific whole class response such as "Can I proceed" by the teacher and "Yes indeed" by students, allows students to get tagged into a teacher's lesson. While, the implementation of this activity within the science class is one that can provide benefits for students' participation in the class, it is not a practice that comes easily if it is engaged in without a respect for students' culture and consistent use. It will also not be as successful when there is not a more general framing of the science classroom as a place where hip-hop culture, is accepted and consistently utilized as a welcome tool for learning.

Haight (2002) mentions that call and response is an integral part of the Black church and also part of the repertoire of successful teachers of African American students. I argue that the effectiveness of call and response is evident in all social fields where participants in hip-hop find themselves, This statement is supported by the fact that those who are a part of hip-hop in places across the globe all utilize call and response in their music. Call-and-response becomes a part of the communal rituals that all of hip-hop engages in. Therefore, it must be part of the in-class approaches to instruction in urban science education. Haight extends her discussion on call-and-response to include the fact that "Within a classroom context, call-and-response sequences may support the cultural values of equality and cultural responsibility among children in contrast to individual competition" (p. 107). This argument supports the fact that the focus on teaching students who are a part of hip-hop should be on the communal bonds they have to each other and not the "individual competition" based traditional approaches to science and science teaching. The science teacher must become part of, or at least have a fundamental understanding of, processes that are staples of the lives of participants in hip-hop. When this occurs, the teacher can easily tag the student into a discussion on science. In essence, the seamlessness of transactions (exchanges of capital where two people or a group of people exchange the knowledge and information they have in order to gain more information) between student and teacher determines the success of rituals that are developed in the classroom that connect students to science. The ideal scenario is that a teacher studies hip-hop culture, engages in conversations with students to validate whether this hip-hop knowledge is accurate, and then concurrently begins conversations with students about science. In these situations, exchanges between student and teacher become so seamless that transactions occur readily. Hip-hop knowledge that the students have is traded for science knowledge that the teacher has, and vice versa. In these scenarios, both parties leave the transactions with more knowledge about each topic discussed than they previously had. If the teacher can consistently make statements that relate to hip-hop, and generate a response from students that breeds positive emotional energy, students' understandings of the subject matter being discussed will develop. In fact, many student rituals that I have observed in science classrooms (whether or not they support the teaching and learning of science) depend upon the relationships students develop with the teacher and other structures in the classroom. The more communal the structures of the classroom, and the more alignment these structures are to hip-hop, the more opportunities there are for transactions between the teacher and student. If the science classrooms are reminiscent of hip-hop fields, students see the teacher as someone who is a part of their community and who has their best interests at heart. They then begin to see classroom learning as a shared endeavor and not a set of activities that is oppositional to their culture.

STUDENT RITUALS AS A KEY TO TRANSACTIONS

Just as certain practices within hip-hop like the rap cypher evolve to become rituals, cogenerative dialogues, which are the rap cyphers of the urban science classroom can also evolve to become rituals when enacted consistently. Cogenerative dialogues are conversations where students and teachers have joint conversations about their experiences inside and outside of classrooms (Tobin & Roth, 2005). The goal of these dialogues is to have conversations about a shared experience with a goal of improving future experiences (Roth et al., 2002). Often beginning with four to six students, but sometimes with just one or to of them and a teacher, these dialogues focus on the science classroom and have the goal of having students and teachers jointly decide upon at least one thing that the group can do to improve subsequent science lessons. These dialogues, when they happen consistently, become "...human ritualized behavior (that) promotes smooth social functioning and does so... by improving communication, channelling aggression and affecting the cohesion of pairs or of groups" (Dissanayake, 1979, p. 29). In the ideal cogenerative dialogues, they are structured like the rap cypher. Participants sit or stand in a circle, take turns speaking, affirm each others sentences by giving eye contact and head nods, and pay close attention to each other. These dialogues, when they become ritualized, become the chief avenue to facilitate transactions between students and teachers in science classrooms just as cyphers facilitate transactions in hip-hop students' lifeworlds.

For example, a student in a high school physics class that I taught repetitively engaged in rituals within the classroom that showed that he was disinterested in the class. He would walk in the classroom with his headphones on, and bring attention to himself whenever the class was quiet by overtly yawning loudly or humming in the class while I taught. The practices he enacted always garnered the attention of his peers and would often distract other students. Eventually, I invited him for lunch after school, and asked if he was willing to engage in a cogenerative dialogue about the classroom. Initially, he declined my invitation. However, after I told him that I was willing to provide extra credit in class in exchange for some of his insight on the class, he agreed.

As soon as he walked in the classroom, his deep connection to hip-hop was unmistakeable. He walked in holding his mp3 player and reciting a rap song. While I initially intended to talk to him about his behavior in class, I picked up on his allegiance to hip-hop and began a discussion on rap by asking him who he was listening to. As the conversation developed, he showed me that he could recite a verse from any rap song that I could mention. At one point, he showed me that he could remember verses from rap songs from any era of hip-hop based on my reciting a few words from an obscure lyric. My interest in his ability to memorize so much information eventually led to a discussion about whether he could utilize his ability to remember information to help him perform better in class. Through this conversation, he showed me that he remembered all of the formulas discussed in the physics class and the concepts that they aligned to. He also made it clear that he knew all the information needed to pass the final exam that was going to be given the next week. As I sat and listened to him describe the main themes in some of the science lessons, the most profound revelation came to me; this student, despite the fact that he appeared not to be, was very interested in the topics being taught in the class. What I perceived as his disinterest in the classroom was actually not that. In fact, his behavior in class was more rooted in his inability to connect to the class, but did not have anything to do with his ability to connect to science. His actions in the classroom, that appeared to be indicative of his feelings about science, were actions in response to the way I was teaching, that eventually developed into rituals. This revelation, and others that came through my dialogues with this student outside of the classroom, drove home the point that when transactions between the hip-hop student and the science classroom are not facilitated, the rituals that students enact will be those that do not function for the benefit of learning and success in the urban classroom.

Therefore, the awareness has to be in place that student rituals within classrooms (particularly those that do not support success in science) may be intentionally enacted and are a part of hip-hops pushing back against structures that deny one voice. "The training... implied by rituals of this kind enables vulnerable groups not only to control their anger but to conduct what amounts to a veiled discourse of dignity and self assertion within public transcript" (Scott, 1990, p. 137). This move towards self-assertion by hip-hop youth functions as a barrier to the students' success in the classroom because they either believe they have to be collectively against a situation by joining a class of their peers in not listening to the teacher, or they inadvertently shut themselves off from opportunities to learn by not paying attention to the teacher. When a student repetitively ignores the teacher's questions in class, does not even look at the teacher when questions are posed in class, or chooses not to attend class at all, these actions are evidence that the structures that have been established in the classroom do not facilitate the fluid exchange of capital within the classroom.

Hundreds of science teachers in urban schools that I have worked with echo the sentiment that the behaviors that students exhibit within the class inhibit them from teaching well. However, only a few of these teachers have been willing to put forth the effort to understand the students' hip-hop culture, study students' rituals or develop rituals of their own that can address the issues they are having with students. Some teachers, who choose to engage in cogenerative dialogues with students in hip-hop, often fail to recognize that the nature of the dialogue, like the cypher, is to grow increasingly more complex and layered as time progresses. In order for this to happen, they must occur consistently. In my work, this involves holding these dialogues at least once a week during lunch or after school. Once these weekly meetings with students happen, they grow more complex in terms of the subject matter being discussed, and become simpler to enact. While they may initially be based on superficial things like the way students sit in class, over time, they naturally progress into more nuanced conversations that surround issues like the nature of science, how and why students' ways of knowing either align with, or are in opposition to the classroom, and how these issues can be addressed in the class-room. The increasingly complex nature of consistently enacted dialogues is similar to the cypher in hip-hop because in the beginning of a cypher, raps are often simple. As the cypher heats up, the complexity in rhyme scheme, metaphor, and analogy increases. Therefore, the progression of the structure of the cogenerative dialogue, and the conversations within it, must grow more complex over time. In fact, if the conversations are remaining similar over time, or if the topics being addressed are consistently the same, this is an indication that things are not going well and that a deeper study of the student culture is necessary before the teacher proceeds with further dialogues.

It is important to note that the initial cogenerative dialogues with students about improving the science classroom may result in the student providing a suggestion for the teacher like "make it more interesting." This occurs because students are still viewing the initial dialogue as an extension of the classroom. In a sense, they are testing the teacher to see if there is a genuine commitment to hearing what the students have to say. However, through discussions with students about the purpose of the dialogue, the teachers laying out the reasons why the student voice is important, and an expression of the teachers effort to learn about the students' culture, the communal nature of the dialogues takes center stage, and rituals that both teachers and students codevelop begin to get formed.

Deconstructing Rituals of Students in Urban Science Classrooms

While the ways that science is taught in urban settings comes from the history of science and the types of curriculum designed for schools that does not necessarily consider whether or not the students are from rural, suburban, or urban settings, the modes of instruction of science are for the most part, rooted in the ways that teachers have been taught, and their expectations of the population they are teaching. Essentially, teachers teach based on their prior experiences both within and outside of the classroom. In the same vein, the actions and rituals of participants in hip-hop are based on an amalgamation of their past and present experiences. For many participants in hip-hop, the rituals they engage in within the classroom are rooted in their experiences as outsiders to a world of opportunity and access that is oftentimes dangled before their eyes, but is perpetually out of reach. For example, many students that I have taught in the Bronx, New York are just a few blocks from the affluence of New York City and can see the skyline of Manhattan from the rooftops of their project buildings in the Bronx. Despite this fact, they feel locked out of possibilities for being part of a world that is only a train ride away. I argue that the ways that these students choose to overcome being locked out of access and opportunity beyond their present is to become defiant. They enact actions like speaking loudly or expressing disinterest in efforts to affirm their strength and mask their vulnerabilities. These actions, over time, develop into types of behavior that become associated with being young, Black and hip-hop.

Through my research in this area of study, I have found that students enact both conscious and unconscious rituals that support their connections to hip-hop, and exclusion from science. In fact, when I have shown videotape from science classrooms to urban students, many of them have been able to identify rituals they have enacted in the classroom and reasons why they enacted them. In some cases, they are able to remember some of their actions, and identify simple reasons why they may have disrupted the classroom such as "I don't like that teacher." In other instances, students did not always realize that they enacted rituals that disrupted the lesson. When these rituals were pointed out to them, their responses were statements that alluded to the fact that educational success in the ways the teacher defined it, was not for them. It seemed to be for those who were part of the world they could see from their rooftops. Therefore, they enacted practices that reflected definitions of success that were misaligned with success in school.

One of the most intriguing rituals that students enacted was walking into the classroom, and then giving each one of their friends a handshake. Students who were late for class often initiated this ritual and always stopped the flow of the lesson when they did so. As I inquired more about this ritual from students, I discovered how insightful they were about the purpose of the ritual and its link to hip-hop. Students were able to share that that the ritual of giving each other a handshake was tied to the fact that respect is one of the most revered and significant parts of hip-hop culture. The students' acknowledgment of their peers in the form of a handshake is a sign of solidarity that signifies their connections to each other, and their disconnections to the outside world.

Within the Black church, this necessity to acknowledge and greet peers is easily seen whenever a member walks in. In fact, within the church, the greeting of peers is so accepted into the formal structure of the service that there is a portion of the traditional Black church service that is dedicated to ensuring that members greet each other. I find that this out of school ritual provides insight into student classroom rituals. Therefore, I argue that by validating this practice, and working with students to ensure that this practice does not interrupt classroom instruction, it can be modified in a way that does not disrupt the lesson or take a significant amount of time away from instruction. For example, in classes that I taught, I would always allow 45 seconds for students to congratulate and greet each other when a question was answered properly, or when the class met a shared goal like getting a high average on a test or assignment. These timed spaces for validation and affirmation of ones peers meets the needs of hip-hop youth and can be part of the structure of the class that signifies that there is a shared notion of success in the classroom.

Lessons from Cogenerative Dialogues About Student Rituals:
Amending and Re-creating Rituals

In one cogenerative dialogue, I invited two students who would take several minutes to greet their peers when they arrived late to class to meet with me during their lunch period. In this conversation, the students were able to tell me that they were consistently late because they wanted to avoid the classroom and a teacher they did not get along with. They also mentioned that sometimes, they took extra time to elaborately greet their peers because they wanted to disrupt the lesson. As the dialogue progressed, the students mentioned that they would do whatever they could to disrupt the class because the teacher "just wanted us (students) to sit and listen for the whole class like some robots. Maybe that's how they do it in them other schools, but that doesn't work here" The fact that the teacher wanted students to sit quietly for the entire class was especially problematic for students because they had to sit quietly during the 80 minute science block that they had once a week. From this conversation, I was able to identify that both of the students were willing to forego learning the subject if it meant that the teacher would not be successful at teaching for the entire class.

After having discussions with students about the fact that being in class on time, and allowing the teacher to have an opportunity to teach was necessary for both the teachers' and their success in science. One of the students then decided, "... We can't keep being late for this class. We have to at least make it on time." Her friend solemnly nodded in response and after the dialogue, the students co-established an amendment to their existent ritual of meeting in the park in the mornings and waiting for class to start before entering the school. Eventually, the teacher was invited to a cogenerative dialogue with the students, and they codeveloped ways to break up the monotony of the 80 minute time block by crating opportunities for students to talk to, and work with, each other.

In another cogenerative dialogue, a student who repeatedly enacted the ritual of putting his head down when he was asked questions in a physics class became aware of this ritual when he and I studied videotape of the class in a cogenerative dialogue. As we both studied videotape of the class, he decided to enact a new practice of maintaining eye contact with the teacher and attempting to answer questions even if he was not quite sure of the answer. By structuring our dialogues to allow for equal opportunities to talk, constant exchanges, and positive affirmation on each others' words, I was able to recreate the structure of the rap cypher and make the student comfortable in being reflective on the practices he enacted in the classroom.

When we returned to the classroom, the student made several conscious moves to enact the new practice we discussed in cogenerative dialogues. Over time, this practice grew into a ritual. In consequent dialogues, he reported that by enacting this new ritual, he felt like teachers and peers began to view him in a different way in the science class. As a result of the success of his newly formed rituals, this student decided that it was important for him to have one of his friends be a part of the cogenerative dialogue or "classroom cypher." Once I began to enact these dialogues with both students, they both began to make suggestions for how they could modify their out of school rituals in ways that support their success in science. One of these new rituals was connecting the physics that they learned in class to videogames that they played outside of school. Before long, both students had matched lessons that were taught in class like Newton's laws of motion, momentum energy and inertia to parts of their basketball and boxing video games.

In a chemistry classroom at the same school where these cogenerative dialogues were enacted, and pushed to become a school ritual, I observed certain students not participating in classroom discussions, having low scores on exams, and exhibiting a general lack of effort in the classroom. These negative actions and behaviors had become ritualized and had become a part of their everyday school practice. Concurrently, these same students were highly engaged in certain after-school activities that involved hip-hop like poetry and dance. In response, I had a conversation with these students to discuss why they were so disengaged in the science classroom, yet actively engaged in other fields. I invited students to have a cypher with me after their science class, and asked them to tell me what was happening in the classroom that caused them not to do well in science. Time and time again during this half an hour discussion, and without going into much detail, students mentioned that they just didn't like the class. After this rather unsuccessful dialogue, I spent a significant amount of time sifting through video recordings of the students' science classes that I had collected. My goal was to use the video to target what it was that specifically turned them off to science. Their response that they just did not like the class was simply not enough.

While I was able to target some specific instances where the students' exchanges with the teacher may have generated their disinterest, I decided to bring the video of the classroom to the students. I loaded the video to my laptop, and then arranged to meet the group of students I had met with the week before. During this dialogue, video clips from the science classroom played in the background like the beat in a rap cypher. This time when they were asked about why they did not engage in class, students responded in much more vivid detail. They took turns speaking and listening and on occasion, began to point out parts of the videotape that they wanted to discuss.

Students began identifying instances where they thought the teacher was "always trying too hard to be tough and yelling for no reason." They also described points where the teacher repetitively enacted specific rituals like raising her voice and only standing at a certain point in the classroom for the entire class period. Finally, they repeatedly identified points when the teacher was "just teaching and not paying attention to the kids." The identification of these teacher rituals within the dialogue led students to invite the teacher to study the video of the class with them.

As the students and their teacher met together and combed through videotape of the chemistry classroom, the teacher was able to identify student rituals that inhibited teaching and learning just as quickly as students identified teacher rituals that inhibited them from connecting to the classroom. Eventually, they both had to learn to achieve their individual goals (to be respected by the students, and to be listened to by the teacher) and concurrently meet larger goals like passing the state exam.

This process of events made it clear that teachers have to find ways to amend the corporate structures of the classroom in order to allow the culture of the students to be welcome in the classroom. Once this happens, students are more likely to amend their existent practices in ways that support positive experiences in the classroom. In other words, both teachers and students have to learn to value each other's capital and make changes to the rituals they express within the classroom. The perceptions that each group holds about the roles and goals of the other have to change if their shared goal of student success in science is to be fully actualized.

Expansion of New Notions of Success

On the journey towards developing successful practices in the science classroom, the first step should be co-defining success with the needs of all parties in the classroom in mind. While the needs of teachers are often met because the power dynamics in the classroom provides them the agency to enact practices that meet their needs, the needs of hip-hop participants are generally not considered. Through my research in urban science classrooms, I find that the two major components of success in the science classroom for hip-hop youth are: first, the ability to understand concepts enough to be able to explain them to someone else; and second, the ability to use or apply the concepts being taught in their everyday lives. When these processes are supported by teachers who allow students to have the space to teach and learn from fellow participants in hip-hop, and when science is taught in ways that are embedded in the nuances of students' culture, mutually sustaining rituals that meet the needs of both students and teachers are developed and teaching becomes meaningful to both the students and the teacher.

MOVING BEYOND THE SILENCE... WE'RE DROPPIN' SCIENCE

As a science education researcher, I get the opportunity to visit science classrooms quite often. Whenever I do, I pay attention to subtle things like school bells, the amount of shuffling in hallways between classes, and how long I hear the sound of chalk dancing across the blackboard in comparison to how long I hear students talking with the teacher about a topic. Just listening to the sounds in the building tells a story about the school, the teachers, the students, the culture of the school, and the extent to which urban youth and teachers have bridged any misalignments that exist between them. As I soak in all of the sounds I hear, answers to questions about the school that don't come from the school administrators come pouring in. Information like whether students are happy to be in the school, whether the science labs are being used to teach science, and whether teachers work hard to connect to students' lives all come from listening to the underlying current of the school that on the surface may seem perfect.

In urban schools, I usually get to the core of what is going on a lot quicker than I do elsewhere. By allowing the sounds of the school to combine with the looks on students' faces, it is easy to identify either disinterest and boredom, or excitement and passion. Just by paying close attention to the interactions between students and their teacher, and the ways they respond to each other, it becomes easy to determine whether or not students are truly learning.

In urban science classrooms when students are tuned in, the way that science is presented allows for their freedom to fall in love with the discipline. The flow of questions is continuous, the quest for questions and answers by students takes prominence over the need to have given questions answered, and the communality expressed through joint cheers, shared tasks, and heated yet civil debates about science are the norm. This type of science instruction features communication among students and teachers that indicate a shared goal and focus, and mirrors the ways that students communicate in hip-hop fields. In this type of science classroom, science talk requires what Newton (2002) describes with elementary school students as "setting the scene" and building the understanding that science is a powerful way of knowing that can be discussed.

In classes where this type of communication does not exist, and students are not tuned in to science, it becomes necessary to purposefully trigger conversations that take on the structure of hip-hop. This is accomplished by studying hip-hop practices, documenting aspects of these practices that may possibly support classroom instruction, and then using information from these practices in the classroom. For example, because call and response is a piece of hip-hop performances, I have worked with teachers on creating call and response cadences in the classroom to get students' attention and generate a focus on the lesson. In other instances, I have encouraged teachers to have students take a minute to greet their peers even if they've been with them all day. Without fail, this approach garners the positive emotions that a teacher needs to begin the process of connecting students to the discipline.

In this chapter, I come to the work as science education researcher, having witnessed both the worst and best case scenarios of instruction in science classes. This is the same stance that I take when I present at education conferences or even present to teachers during professional development sessions. The only difference is that when I have presented at conferences or schools in the past, I have purposefully excluded the fact that the successful initiatives I have used to connect urban youth to science have been based on hip-hop. Despite the fact that hip-hop has consistently been a major theme in my work, I often ended up extracting hip-hop from the crux of my arguments about improving urban science education. This was the case because in many scholarly arenas, I felt pressure to meet the needs or expectations of audiences that reacted negatively towards any initial slant towards hip-hop in my academic work. This audience did not see beyond the negative associations that have been tied to hip-hop culture long enough to allow for an intellectual argument that supports the use of hip-hop in the science classroom. In response, I unintentionally weakened the arguments I was making in efforts to please an academic audience.

As I have continued to conduct my research in urban science classrooms, and have consistently heard students describe themselves as hip-hop or witnessed them engage in hip-hop, I have come to realize that extracting hip-hop from the arguments I make about urban science education undermines their potential for my research to effect change in urban science classrooms. Furthermore, it weakens the effectiveness of the resources and ideas I have developed that can benefit the teaching and learning of science for students who are most marginalized from science. At this stage in my research, and at this point in the body of work provided by urban science educators, I have come to realize that it is important to address the needs of marginalized urban youth by focusing on science education research that is hip-hop based and inspired.

In these two final chapters, I wrap up the arguments being made in this book by tying together the major themes I have presented thus far. I do so by re-grounding the work in the reasons why hip-hop based science education is necessary for urban youth. I undertake this task by describing the lifeworlds of the hip-hop generation and showing how what is traditionally viewed as the urban students experience is oftentimes a more superficial layer of the hip-hop experience. This re-analysis of the urban experience, particularly in regards to the science classroom, is a key step in beginning to better understand how to reach those who are most marginalized from science achievement.

The misidentification of participants in hip-hop as "just the urban student" results in the misdirection of science pedagogy and limits the effectiveness of approaches to instruction that researchers develop. By this, I mean that pedagogy is often designed to meet the wrong goals because it is focused on the needs of a generalized urban student identity that is not representative of the more pervasive population that identifies itself as hip-hop. The generalized urban focus that we see in urban science education, that does not consider hip-hop, overemphasizes the focus on the urban student as city resident. Hence, it is more focused on the urban context as location rather than as culture. The difference between the more conventional approach to urban science instruction and the type that focuses less on location and more on culture is the pedagogical approach that each one breeds. Traditional urban science education focuses on the fact that the school is located in an urban setting and in many instances overemphasizes the ethnic and racial divides within the school at the expense of the shared culture of the youth in school. This becomes another cause for the division between the way students see themselves and the way the institutions see them. Science becomes an avenue through which deficit views of urban youth become transmitted and an extension of the corporate institutions that limit agency. For example, the language of hip-hop, which is often a vernacular form of English is constantly devalued in science and leads to what Montgomery (2004) refers to as a linguistic imperialism in science that does not consider the potential of ways of talk other than standard English in scientific descriptions or explanations. Without work that considers an ethnically inclusive discourse like hip-hop, such as that of Brown (2006), the science classroom serves as a space to inhibit students from talking science across ethnic divides through their shared hip-hop talk. I name the approach to urban science education that focuses more on the culture of the urban setting (and therefore, the language, schema and practices), as Reality pedagogy.

Reality pedagogy, which is teaching that considers student culture and cultural artifacts in the delivery of science content, does not focus on naming students as urban just for the sake of associating them with a context. It focuses less on what the student looks like, how the student behaves, and how to control this behavior, and more on understanding who the student is, and immersing oneself so deeply in urban youth culture that it becomes second nature to develop their interest in, and enhance their natural affinity for, science. Implementing approaches to teaching that are developed for the urban student, and not for the hip-hop student, obscures the teachers ability to see the urban hip-hop student's ability to learn. In response, the student's hip-hop identity -that shows vulnerability, a desire to learn, and a responsibility for others, becomes masked by perceptions of who they are perceived to be as urban students. Rather than support student interest in the discipline, traditional approaches to instruction call forth an urban student identity that is marked by exhibitions of indifference and a lack of interest in school and science.

Rituals and transactions in Hip-hop

The hip-hop lifeworld, like the urban student experience, is a complex set of interconnected and identifiable rituals. In hip-hop, the live performance, the nature of the cypher, the development of rap and dance crews, (b-boying, getting lite, wu-tanging) are pieces of the culture that can be studied for deeper insight into ways to improve instruction. The call and response seen in every rap show, where the emcee engages in a rousing call and response with the audience, the celebratory freeze after a breaking performance, and the inclusion of a crew/entourage in supporting the artist during a rap performance are each rituals that function to affirm the communality in hip-hop. Each of these rituals stands in contrast to the harsh, gang member, and delinquent urban youth personas that traditional urban pedagogy is geared towards.

In the hip-hop participant's life, rituals like the ones mentioned in the previous paragraph often develop into collective responses to either physical or symbolic structures that do not allow them to engage in exchanges with each other. In other instances, the rituals enacted by urban youth are an affirmation of the ties that connect participants in hip-hop to each other. For example, there is a distinct loud noise that is made up to a window or to a person around a street block that is commonly heard in urban settings. The making of this sound is an action that necessitates a distinct response by a peer. It is a ritual that is enacted so that all people involved in the exchange know that they are communicating with each other. In addition, when rap artists are performing at a show and say, "When I say ____ you say ____," the artists are calling out to the audience to ensure that the crowd is willing to exchange with them. The crowd's response determines the type of performance that is given and lets the performer know whether there is a connection between the audience and the artist.

The types of exchanges that indicate that a connection exists among participants require such a fluid exchange of capital that the two participants/groups who are involved in the exchange are often not conscious of the fact that they are engaging in it. In the event that they become conscious of the process they are engaging in, the main goal of the participants is to ensure that all persons involved in the exchange are tuned in to each other and prepared to engage in future transactions.

In my studies, I find that the rituals enacted by students who are a part of hip-hop are set forth with the expectation of feedback. In essence, hip-hop rituals are often efforts to transact with others. They are enacted with a goal of attaining some type of reciprocity. Even in the science classroom, hip-hop students are always striving to engage in transactions with both their peers and the teacher. Unfortunately, when these attempts to transact are enacted within the classroom, they are misread. For example, when students in the classroom know an answer to a question in class, and begin to almost jump out of their seats or speak loudly in order to get the teacher's attention. The teacher may view the students' behavior as a distraction rather than an attempt to engage in a transaction. The excited response of the student to a teachers question is analogous to the distinct yell on the corner by the participant in hip-hop who is waiting for a response from a friend who is in a building window or around a corner. The hip-hop students' expectations in the classroom scenarios are to get a response that acknowledges that they are heard and that there is a space to exchange. However, if the teacher misreads these cues, the student's needs are not met and an exchange does not occur. In my previous research, I find that a repetitive effort to transact that is not met will often result in situations where students either choose not to participate, or choose to engage in transactions with someone other than the teacher. In these instances, the hip-hop student may hear what is going on in the classroom, may be partly conscious of what is going on in the class, but will not transact with the teacher. In instances where these regressions of transactions occur, the ways that the student and the teacher communicate can be called a "fundamental interaction."

Scientifically, a fundamental interaction is a force that exists between particles that does not encompass a true exchange. In fact, particles in a fundamental interaction only exchange virtual particles but not real ones. When students who are a part of hip-hop are engaged in fundamental interactions in the urban science classroom, they are physically in the classroom, but are not truly exchanging capital with the structures of the classroom. In a sense, a pseudo exchange (like the exchange of virtual particles) occurs where students are in the classroom, may be listening to the teacher, but are not receiving any true information from, or sending any information to, the teacher.

In conversations I have had with students in physics, chemistry and biology classes over the course of a four-year study, students were able to describe many scenarios where they were only superficially engaging with the teacher. These occasions typically arose when students felt excluded from the classroom and were not interested in the classroom or the lesson even though they were in the class and may have even appeared to be paying attention. One student described the process as when students would be "sitting quietly in the classroom but not paying any attention to the teacher."

Varela (1999) refers to actions such as these as "immediate coping." These are situations where individuals develop reactions to scenarios they are facing in order to immediately deal with them. The development of the persona of the prototypical urban student that does not have an interest in science or education is the culmination of many immediate coping mechanisms for dealing with classrooms where students feel like they cannot actively participate in the science classroom or that their attempts to do so are repetitively rebuffed by the teacher.

Conversely, students whose efforts to transact in a classroom are supported by teachers, enact rituals that support teaching and learning. With these students, rituals such as paying close attention to someone who is speaking, arriving to class on time, and seamlessly responding to, and asking questions in the classroom become the norm. Classrooms where these positive transactions are enacted stand in contrast to traditional urban classrooms where rituals such as students putting their head down in class, turning away from their teachers when they speak, coming to class late, or disrupting the class, are the norm.

If that's your man, then tag him in: From Corporate to Communal Classrooms

In Harlem, New York, the phrase "if that's your man, then tag him in" used by hip-hop dancers provides an example of how participants in hip-hop transact. In this process, a person showcases dance moves and goes back and forth with a peer who is either learning the dance, or displaying a new move. Each person showcases a few dance steps, and then tags another person into the process until all the people within the social field get an opportunity to be involved in teaching, learning or just demonstrating a dance move. Each time that I have witnessed this process being enacted, I quickly become engrossed in the spirit of togetherness among the youth. They sacrifice their space in the limelight to ensure that others learn, they transition from student to teacher seamlessly, and they communicate with each other in both verbal and non-verbal ways. Within the tagging in process, when a person is doing a dance move that does not look like it is part of the dance being taught, it is not discarded. Rather, it is incorporated into the dance move being taught and used as a part of the teaching and learning. Through my observations of the types of exchanges in hip-hop dance, a lot of information about the communal nature of teaching and learning are uncovered.

I argue that urban science classrooms are places where communal practices like the "tagging in" process enacted by participants in hip-hop can take root. In the science class, this process could involve a teacher conducting an experiment or solving a problem in front of the class, and then being willing to allow students to become part of the process by having them come to the front of the class to complete experiments and problems. This tagging in process also allows students to tag in peers to assist them when they are solving problems either at the board. In this process, whether the student gets a question right or not, there is a space provided to tag another student in to the process. When this process occurs on a regular basis in the classroom, it can become a ritual that allows the science class to become a communal space where everyone in the classroom has a role to play in helping each other meet their collective goals. In the exchanges that occur within communal classrooms, students move toward full understanding of science because their non-science knowledge is valued, and then used to support their learning of science. Even when students do not get an answer right, or have questions that don't necessarily relate to the specific science topic that is presently being discussed, the information they provide is accepted and utilized in a way that supports instruction. In this process, the teacher understands that the acceptance of hip-hop culture in the classroom allows for multiple opportunities for students to connect to science. Therefore, the teacher's task is to capitalize on the students' attempts to connect to the classroom and find ways to connect these attempts to science.

Based on the outcomes of my research on how structures from hip-hop can support communal urban classrooms, and my study of students' group decisions on what is communal, I find that there are many simple ways that the classroom can be structured in a way that supports communal practices. This includes allowing students to sit in proximity to each other, creating opportunities for them to help each other to study, creating the space within classrooms for sharing experiences that relate to the topic at hand, and allowing students to show understanding by talking through the steps of a problem with someone who may not understand.

When Communal Classrooms don't happen

When communal practices are not a part of what happens in urban classrooms, the classroom can be described as corporate. These types of classrooms are rigid in structure and follow a format where the needs and desires of hip-hop youth are not considered in the instruction. For example, if students think it is important to show how much they understand science content by teaching their peers and having informal conversations about what they know, a corporate understanding would be a process where teachers inhibit students from enacting these practices. For example, in a corporate classroom, students' knowledge of a science topic may be assessed only through a test or exam when they would rather show what they know by presenting to the class, interpreting their content knowledge through art or performance, or through portfolios. When the structures of the corporate classroom truncate students' opportunities to display their knowledge, their willingness to transact are limited, and they are more likely to exhibit behaviors that do not support their own learning.

In a set of video vignettes of urban science classrooms collected over the course of four years, there were many scenarios where teachers repetitively spent a majority of the class period teaching without giving students much opportunity to ask questions or engage in discussions about what was being taught. Many students would sit and look towards the front of the class, would rarely talk, but would appear seemingly attentive. This type of class is the prototypic corporate classroom. On the surface, the classes appeared to be well organized, and the students within the class could be described as quiet and attentive. However, student participation and poor grades indicated that the students were not connecting to science in this corporate setting.

When video from these classrooms were shown to the students who were not doing well in science, they described the many video vignettes they were presented with as examples of what goes on in most of their classrooms. One of the students described a video clip where a teacher seemed to keep teaching while he was attempting to get her attention to share some insight on the topic. When asked about what was going during the video clip, he mentioned that the video was one of many instances "when the teacher is talking and talking (teaching a lesson) and we're (all students in the class) all just sitting there in another world."

About a week later, a conversation with the teacher in the video vignette described above revealed what the teacher's perspective was on the same event. as one where she successfully averted a students' attempt to disrupt the lesson. She then described the entire situation as an example of students "...who just don't care about their education."

In order to make sense of the differences in the student and teachers' perspectives on the same video vignette, I decided to study each of them more closely. Despite what the teacher said, it appeared to me that the student wanted to be successful in the classroom. In addition, despite the student's perspectives of the teacher, it appeared that she was well intentioned, and wanted them to succeed. I began by visiting the teacher for two class periods a day for two months. I took detailed notes on her teaching, the ways she structured her classroom, and the way that she communicated with students. I also engaged in further conversations with her about her students, and what she identified as "the challenges of teaching urban kids." This more focused study of the teacher revealed that the teacher was truly concerned about the students' learning of science. In the classroom, she repetitively mentioned what students from more affluent schools could do, that the students in her class couldn't. When questioned about this practice, she spoke with passion about her desire to prepare students for the real world, and "shake off the apathy" that the students had about school. However, she also spoke about the fact that "students need structure and a teacher that doesn't let them get away with anything." In one instance she said, "Science is not easy, it requires discipline, they may not like it (the way I teach) now, but they will eventually want to learn." From the teacher's last statement, it was apparent that she felt that her modes of instruction would eventually lead to the students' interest in science and passing the class.

In addition to my focus on the teacher, I spent a lot of time studying students' discussions about school when they were in close proximity to their friends and enacting hip-hop practices (such as rapping in lunchrooms, freestyling in a local park, and interacting with each other in the neighborhood of the school). While documenting students' conversations with their peers in these places, I was able to identify that when they were not in the classroom, under the watchful eye of the teachers, they consistently spoke about being successful in school, their interest in passing their classes, and in one particularly telling conversation, the fact that being passive and disengaged in the classroom was what the teacher wanted from them. From this conversation, it was apparent that these students, who enacted many hip-hop practices on a regular basis, wanted to learn, and wanted to do well in their science class. They recalled a few sentences that the teacher made in class related to the chemistry of creating soaps, chemicals, and flammable substances that they were interested in but that they did not explore in class. Contrary to their teachers' opinion, they were far from apathetic towards school. However, because the structures within the classroom did not facilitate students' transactions within the classroom, they felt like they needed to be disengaged.

After analyzing all of my conversations with teachers and students, I was able to conclude that the teachers' enactment of corporate practices in order to get students to be interested in success in school were useless because students were already interested. What the classroom needed was more communal structures in the classroom so that student interest in school and science could be readily expressed.

The types of scenarios described above are examples of prevalent, yet overlooked moments in the lives of hip-hop students. It is symbolic of the many situations where the teacher perceives students as disinterested in the classroom, when they are actually looking for opportunities to get involved. These are the moments that precede the students' decision to express their dissatisfaction with the existing approaches to instruction in the classroom. Misperception of hip-hop youth is the seedbed for their dissatisfaction with schooling. This dissatisfaction may be expressed as being passive or quiet, or being extremely vocal and excited. In either type of situation, the students are awaiting opportunities where they can be "tagged in" by the teacher in a way that is comparable to when they are tagged in to communal practices in hip-hop. The moments in the classroom where hip-hop youth are not tagged in to the classroom are the same moments where they turn away from schools and science and begin to develop distaste for schools, science, or both. This distaste for science is similar to the feelings that many of these students have for other institutions within their community such as the police. Police brutality and unjust arrests and harassment become paralleled with the teacher who does not allow the student to have a voice or to participate. For example, a student in a science class who asks the teacher if they can perform a lab experiment, and who is responded to by the teacher with a statement like "that lab is for the advanced students only" – as was the case in a biology class I visited in a school in Harlem, New York City, becomes not only turned off to the teacher, but to science. The entire existence of hip-hop students then becomes a set of experiences where there is a division between the way they see the world, and the ways that institutions that perpetuate another vision of the world does. Science becomes an extension of the corporate institutions that limit agency and school becomes a space that houses students for a couple of hours in the day and not an institution that is supposed to help them to succeed. In response, participants in hip-hop react to science in the same way that they do when being insulted in the media, or denied resources to fully participate in social and political arenas. They create their own versions of reality where they are free from those who have oppressed them. They create their own science.

CREATING A HIP-HOP SCIENCE

Hip-hop science has its roots in the religious belief system of the "5 percenter Islamic sect" which was an offshoot of the Nation of Islam. The 5 percenters began in the early 1960s in Harlem, New York. They saw themselves as the 5 percent of the Black population who have "knowledge of self" and understand the strength of Blacks in the United States. The group used the words science and mathematics to describe the logic behind the experiences of the marginalized Black-American populace and provided daily "lessons" for their followers based on their unique understandings of science and mathematics. The 5 percenters use their science as a way to use their astute observations about Black life to present information that followers can use to improve their subjugated status in the United States. The use of the words science and mathematics by the 5 percenters was absorbed into hip-hop, which was created a few miles away from Harlem in the Bronx in the 1970s. As a result of hip-hop's commitment to providing a voice for Black Americans, and the alignment of this goal to the 5 percenters' goal of uplifting Blacks, the word "science" became merged into, and a key part of, hip-hop. Sapienza (2004) in her work with scientific researchers identifies being well-informed, persistent, flexible/ open to new ideas, and autonomous (rejecting external regulations) as attributes of creative scientists. These are the same attributes that the 5 percenters exhibited as they created a hip-hop science. In addition, They realized the same things that good science educators do, such as the fact that the extent to which depth in science is taught, is related to how relevant the instructors feel it relates to the life experiences of students (Lincoln, 1994). The 5 percenters could connect Astronomy to Muslim countries and in nations that are historically populated by people of color, and then used this fact to make their students interested in studying, and experts in the discipline.

Hip-hop, Science and the Cypher: Connecting Culture and Practice

In contemporary hip-hop, studies of science went beyond astronomy. For example, the lyric, "Dealing in my cypher, I revolve around sciences" was on a song entitled Criminology by rap artists Ghostface Killah and Raekwon in 1995. The song was one of the most popular on the underground hip-hop scene at the time, and had an infectious beat that caught my attention. There was something intriguing about the fact that the artists of the song were using words like criminology and science to describe hip-hop. On the song, the artists play on the fact that criminology is the science of crime and attribute the general notions of intelligence, preciseness and accuracy that are used to describe criminologists to themselves. When Ghostface identifies the cypher (which are social spaces where participants in hip-hop communicate with each other – which have been discussed throughout this work) and the fact that science is what his cypher revolves around, he alludes to the fact that there is a brand of science that is purely hip-hop. His words show that within the spaces where the artist is in direct communication with fellow participants in the culture, the words being spoken are based on a hip-hop science. This science is based on the ability to look for, and provide precise answers to, questions and deliver sharp and accurate descriptions of life in the "inner city" that will resonate with all that similarly experience the rituals that make up the life of the participant in hip-hop.

Since the song's release in 1995, the part of the lyric that says, "I revolve around science/s" has been sampled and/or repeated by many artists. Most notably, they have been used by rappers like Mos Def and Planet Asia who are arguably in a league of the most prolific rappers on their respective coasts of the United States. These artists use Raekwon and Ghostface's phrase to display what they see as the science in their everyday experiences and the precision they take in creating their raps, the exactness of their rhyme patterns, the complexities of the subject matter they discuss and the uniqueness in their delivery. In the song Mathematics, where Mos Def (1999) uses the phrase "It's simple mathematics...I revolve around science," he makes a connection between science and mathematics and utilizes numerical data about topics that range from the low minimum wage in the United States to the jail sentencing of people of color to be a part of his version of science. The numerical data that he uses become the tools through which he can combine mathematics and hip-hop science. Just as scientific formulas combine science and math in canonical science. The chorus to the song showcases the ways that hip-hop artists use science and mathematics in ways that mean something to participants in the culture, and varies from the way these constructs are used in schools. Planet Asia (2000), who uses the phrase from Ghostface and Raekwon, defines his view of science as having a focus on "dedication to the skill to say what you feel" and "keeping it street, just to eat." In other words, being scientific in this arena requires dedication, skill and genuineness to oneself and the environment where one comes from.

The word "science" is also prominently used in hip-hop through the phrase "droppin' science." In this phrase science takes on a different meaning because the phrase droppin' science refers to a rap where an individual engages in a descriptive, multilayered, and complex use of words that relays the ontologies of marginalized urban youth while it dismisses conventional notions of what is good or smart as defined by school. Through an analysis of the phrase droppin' science and the way it is used by participants in hip-hop, it becomes evident that science in hip-hop is scientific; in the sense that it caries forth a central theme of science that seeks to answer unknown questions and provide multilayered descriptions of certain phenomena in systematic ways that grow increasingly complex. Hip-hop science describes natural phenomena, recants the rituals engaged in by participants in hip-hop, and invites transactions while providing evidence (through words) and visual arts that supports an argument being made by an artist. Along this line of thought, a hip-hop verse, can be likened to a scientific presentation, in that it includes an overview or a review of previous work and then expands into the new discoveries of the scientist. For example, Tupac (1998) cites Huey Newton and then proceeds to lay out his own quest for changes in the Black community. Since then, other rappers have cited Tupac and enacted hip-hop science by outlining their own innovative approaches to looking at life in urban settings.

In rap music, "dropping science" or "droppin' science" involves the use of complex rhyme patterns and wordplay. The art of "dropping science" is as complex as it is subjective and oftentimes describes how urban youth view themselves as being locked into spaces that forces beyond them place them in. For example, Killah Priest of the rap group Wu Tang Clan in a song titled Science Project describes how the housing projects in New York City seem like a scientist's project (Killah Priest, 1990). He describes the experience of living in housing projects (places of residence for socioeconomically disadvantaged populations) as an existence that feels like scientists are conducting experiments on the lives of the urban youth who live within them. Through his descriptions, he drops science by discussing, describing, predicting, and analyzing a number of situations he has witnessed as a resident of these housing projects. This ability to discuss, describe, predict, and analyze are necessary skills for being a part of both hip-hop and being a traditional scientist. However, the ability to drop science as a participant in hip-hop is not considered an attribute that is necessary for involvement in, or the learning of, science within schools. The lack of consideration for the skill set that participants in hip-hop possess is responsible for the term "droppin' science" and the Socratic and literal irony that the term evokes. Droppin' science in hip-hop can be interpreted as a process where science as we know it, or as it is taught within schools, is literally made to drop or fall to a lower position relative to the scientific understandings of urban youth. Being hip-hop then means being able to concurrently drop traditional science and create your own.

Unfortunately, science is presented to students in schools as one of the fundamental disciplines that explains life, and "when an area of intellectual activity is tagged with the label 'science' people who are not scientists are de facto barred from having any say about its substance" (Jasanoff, 1991, p. 14). For participants in hip-hop, the separation of their existences from school, their inability to transact within the science classroom, and their ability to engage in a hip-hop science means that they do not have to be a part of conventional science. A rap group who names itself "Self Scientific," makes a statement that participants in hip-hop do not need to be validated by institutions that name a person as scientific because they have the ability to name themselves as scientific. This naming of self as scientific is a demand to be seen as intellectually capable and is an effort to change the common perception among teachers that rap music and hip-hop culture are superficial or non intellectual. It is also an opportunity to define oneself as not only outside of traditional science, but also above it.

For many urban youth who are participants in hip-hop, choosing to define one self as a part of the culture often results in the ostracizing of self from the alienating structures that too often exist in other arenas such as schools. Consequently, the choice to become a part of hip-hop, embrace the culture, and immerse oneself in it becomes a choice to be part of a world where one is central and has a say in the decisions that are made within the culture rather than an insignificant piece of a larger world where one has no voice. Oftentimes, science presents itself as one of the fields where a participant in hip-hop would feel like an insignificant piece of the world. This is the case because it is presented as a discipline that is reserved only for a small group of people who make all the decisions for everyone else. The small group that makes the decisions is perceived to be the traditional scientist (White male wearing a lab coat that almost all students draw when prompted to draw a picture of a scientist) that makes all the decisions for all the people. By the people, I refer to people from varying ethnic backgrounds that populate urban areas. However, I speak more specifically about hip-hop youth who have been made to feel that the "special ability" or necessary intelligence to engage in science is out of their reach. This is why they create spaces of their own through hip-hop, and a science through rap that drops conventional science.

The creation of a new approach to science or a new way of analyzing and understanding the world through rap is in itself a science that reshapes what conventional science is. This fact leads to the major difference between science as it is used in conventional discourse and science in hip-hop discourse. In hip-hop, one of the major goals of engaging in science or creating/dropping science is that the science is just as relatable as it is complex. Despite the fact that the person that "drops science" is valued and possesses an ability that is uncommon because it requires a specific kind of skill, the relatability of the rap to the layperson is important. This leads to a significant point in the separation of hip-hop science from school science. In hip-hop science, the rapper that doesn't have an intimate relationship with an audience is not effective but the science teacher that does not reach the students or connect to their experiences is all-too-often still valued and respected. The divisions between these two types of science (hip-hop and school) lies in the fact that school science is structured to not accept or support new ways of knowing or doing, but rather, focuses on the indoctrination of people into the established culture of canonical science. This fact positions science, and in many cases, school, as a way to lose individuality and another avenue through which the participant in hip-hop loses her voice.

A focus on the standpoint of those who are a part of hip-hop culture, and an observation of the attributes that they exhibit, provides insight on the fact that students who are engaged in the culture possess creative and "outside of the box" attributes such as unique abilities to vividly describe or explain in detail what school science doesn't allow for. The lack of value for these hip-hop generated attributes and a lack of recognition for the hip-hop generations' ability to make contributions to science is evident in any examination of curricula in urban schools and the absence of references to contemporary urban social issues that can possibly connect students from urban settings into science. As this process continues, students who do not have examples to connect them to science have no reference points or areas of expertise to use as leverage into the world of science. Through the institutionalized barring of their culture within schools, hip-hop youth are inhibited from using the science knowledge they do have, and are withheld from using the tools they have for obtaining new knowledge. Consequently, they engage in a search for what Coburn (2005?) refers to as "cognitive authority" and reach for whatever it is that can provide them with an opportunity to display their knowledge and demonstrate their ideas.

In the book Street Science, Coburn (2005) mentions the fact that disadvantaged groups within urban areas are rejecting the notion that science or scientific thinking should be left to professional scientists who exclude them from the scientific process. In response, and in a search for "cognitive authority," they develop a street science, which is reflective of hip-hop's science in the ways that it drops traditional science. Street science "re-values forms of knowledge that professional science has excluded [and] democratizes the inquiry and decision making process" (Coburn, 2005, p. 3). For hip-hop, the effort to democratize the inquiry and decision making process not allowed for in the science classroom involves the creation of new social fields that provide opportunities for full participation. Since science achievement and the ability to express scientific ability and self concept are related (Lau, Yeung & Jin, & Low, 1998) and self-concept as scientific or intelligent is only allowed to flourish outside of schools, there is a legitimate reason for why urban youth who are a part of hip-hop choose not to achieve in science classrooms that do not affirm their intelligence.

When students become a part of hip-hop and become affirmed for their abilities to drop science within contexts outside of schools, they begin to become more astute about the role of schools and schooling in their lives. As they get exposed to more science classes in schools and begin to notice that people from other cultures become larger pieces of science while they continually do not see themselves, they begin to see the subjectivity and bias behind what is presented as science in schools. It then becomes perfectly clear why students spend hours engaging in hip-hop activities like writing graffiti, perfecting raps and creating anti-institution hip-hop personas at the expense of spending their time and energy to become a part of science. The fuller their immersion in hip-hop, the more complex their observations about life and institutions like schools are. The more complex their life experiences are, the more aware they are of the fact that canonical science and its contemporary explications are rooted in a pro-western and anti-hip-hop ideology. Before long, the questions the science teacher asks, the limitations and boundaries of cookbook lab experiments, the simplistic interpretations of these experiments, and the pre-drawn conclusions that arise from corporate approaches to teaching science become more and more inconsequential. In essence, hip-hop either becomes the means through which we support urban students' engagement in science (when we embrace it), or the avenue through which hip-hop youth drop school science for a science of their own (when it is not considered in the teaching and learning of science).

CHAPTER 9

REFRAMING URBAN SCIENCE EDUCATION

Practical Tools and Ideological Perspectives

REDISCOVERING THE HOOD: ENACTING REALITY PEDAGOGY

For those who are part of hip-hop culture, what they require is an approach to instruction that presents an avenue through which their realities are given voice and their potential to inform their own teaching and learning is released. I suggest that the primary means through which the work outlined throughout this book affects change in urban science education is Reality Pedagogy. Reality Pedagogy extends beyond any existent approach to educating hip-hop youth because it not only focuses on where a person stands within distinct social fields but how that person maneuvers through these fields. It brings artifacts from hip-hop culture into the classroom but also focuses on the skills and talents an individual is afforded because of being positioned as other than the norm. It considers cultural relevance, but takes that approach a bit further by requiring the teachers' cultural immersion and constant ingestion of the cultural outputs of the students' culture. It requires reading, listening to, observing, learning from, and then teaching.

I arrived at this approach to science instruction through my experiences as a middle school science and mathematics teacher about ten years ago. I had lived not too far from the school a few years before I took the job and was reluctant to take it because the school was in a "tough neighborhood." After my first few days of teaching, I quickly realized that my past connection to the neighborhood was an asset that benefited me more than I could have ever imagined.

After one of my first few days of teaching, a student from the school recognized me as someone who had played basketball with his older brother a few years ago. Students were surprised that a teacher actually played basketball in the neighborhood and were more respectful and attentive to me than they were just a few days earlier. Because of my relationship with this student, and the advantages it provided me, I decided to rebuild connections to many of the people from the neighborhood. One of these connections was to a school aide who lived in the projects across the street from the school. He was instrumental in everything from the organization of after-school programs to helping teachers deal with classroom management issues. He invited me to his birthday celebration in the housing projects where he came from and where about 95% of the students I taught lived. It was a welcome invitation and I was excited to get an opportunity to get a closer look at the place where so many of my students came from. I had lived just outside the neighborhood many years ago, but it had been awhile since being in that environment and I had lost touch with what the students' experiences were.

First stop, Third Avenue

I pulled up to a curb right off Third Avenue in the Bronx, saw a small crowd with faces that I recognized, got out of my car, and walked towards them. I greeted all the familiar faces, and was introduced to those I didn't recognize. We all exchanged handshakes that pulled into slight hugs, and began to walk towards the sound of a rap song that was playing on a radio in the small playground in the middle of the housing projects. There were no fancy decorations and no birthday cake, but there was an air of celebration that filled the night. We laughed, joked and toasted to the celebrant who had reached a milestone by turning 25. At about midnight, as the group settled at a small park in the middle of the housing projects, I realized that many students from the school walked past. Some waved hello, gave a head nod, and walked on. Others looked either surprised or confused to see me sitting on the chipped paint covered bench in the middle of the projects. In most cases, students smiled in ways that showed that they appreciated that I was there. In a few cases, they joined the celebration by taking seats on one of the benches, and joined in on some of the conversations.

At one point, two of my students walked up, gave all the men gathered a handshake, and joined the initial group sitting on the benches. In the middle of the playground, in the wee hours of the morning, Black and Latino/a men and women from ages 14–30 sat together talking about music, discussing the cameras that had just been put into the building lobbies to police the residents in the neighborhood, and rapping along with the song that played over the radio. One of the older brothers in the cypher stopped to ask the younger guys how they were doing in school. They both looked around to avoid the question as I tried to explain that they weren't doing their best but had the potential to do much better.

As I began speaking, I was interrupted by three or four loud pops. The group of people who had gathered quickly reacted to the gunshots. Some ducked behind benches or ran towards the nearby building. Some people stood on the benches trying to see where the shots were coming from. One of my students ducked behind a bench next to me and asked if I was okay. As all of this happened, everyone was completely quiet as the music from the nearby radio continued to play. As the song came to an end, a still silence pierced the air. I slowly peered from the space between the two wood blocks that made up the back of the bench to see if it was safe to move. Before long, the air was filled once again as another song started playing on the radio. I looked up to see the crowd that just scattered slowly gathering together again. I had thought the night was over, but after a quick joke about how a few gunshots couldn't stop a party, we returned to our celebration.

A toast was raised, speculations about who might have started shooting went back and forth, and the conversation shifted to the younger members of the group. We returned to our earlier discussion about their performance in school, and the younger members of the group were admonished for their lack of effort in school. They responded to being admonished with a high level of respect for the older members of the group, and shared their frustrations with school and promised to work harder. The older members of the group talked about the frustrations they had when they were in school, and then told the younger group the challenges they were currently experiencing because they did not have an education. As the older group members gave honest advice, and the younger group attentively listened, I couldn't help but notice the deep level of care and compassion for each other that the entire group exhibited. This collective caring or communality was indicative of the entire group's collective hip-hopness.

Second Stop: Back to School

When I returned to the school the next week, my experience that Saturday was still vivid. It had been such an eye opening experience that I had to make it the focus of my instruction. I mentioned the street I drove up to in an example in class about the speed of cars driving down a street, mentioned the names of people I had met from the neighborhood as examples instead of the names in the textbook, and even talked about the shooting that happened during the weekend. Students responded by paying close attention when I spoke, sharing their own examples, and being so deeply engaged in the lesson that I realized that not putting myself in a position to understand their realities, and not bringing these types of experiences into the classroom, meant that I was not teaching to the best of my ability. While an explicit focus on how I have captured students realities in teaching through practical tools will be interrogated in another project, a key point for the reader who does not have access to the types of student experiences that I have described above, is the focus on being honest with students about ones experiences. I argue that a description of ones own experiences, and a use of these experiences in teaching is as valuable as shared experiences with students like the one I described.

After watching students who never had anything to say in the classroom, all of a sudden become interested, and seeing students who usually participated engage in ways I never could have imagined by coming with up with examples from their experiences that related to science topics, I realized that under normal circumstances, students had to subdue parts of their hip-hop identity, or ignore their experiences that could support their learning in order to be considered a "good science student." I had to learn that there are parts of the students' hip-hop identities that are conducive to, and supportive of, success in science. However, without an exposure to students' hip-hop lifeworlds, and an understanding of their experiences - that comes with immersing myself in their realities, I may have never fully come to this realization.

For teachers, it is necessary to understand how students know, feel and experience the world by becoming familiar with where students come from and consciously immersing oneself in their culture. This immersion in student culture, even for teachers who may perceive themselves to be outsiders to hip-hop, simply requires taking the time to visit, observe, and study student culture. Exposing oneself to hip-hop students' lives requires becoming a part of, or a student of, the communities that hip-hop youth come from, and being inquisitive about what makes them who they are. On some basic level, just letting students know that you care about them, sharing with them that you don't know how to reach them, and being comfortable with discussing the steps you have taken to learn about them, are fundamental first steps for reaching them.

For those who are not hip-hop, but who have gotten to the point where they can see the purpose of using it as a tool for connecting urban youth to school and science, the realization that there is a vision into teaching and learning that marginalized populations possess that teachers may not have, must be the driving theme of their instruction. For these teachers, letting hip-hop youth know that the tools that they come to the classroom with are valued within the classroom is necessary. This may require being perceived as disingenuous by students, or pandering to hip-hop youth by others within the school. However, it is important to deal with the discomfort that comes with losing the power that the teacher has as the leader of the class-room, and realizing that the larger goal is to make an impact on the lives of hip-hop youth. Over time, with a consistent search for, understanding of, and respect for the students' culture, students appreciate the teacher's effort to transact, and work with the teacher to develop a hip-hop based approach to instruction. In addition, the success that a teacher has in regards to classroom management and student success on exams and other forms of assessment pacifies the dissent that others within school and education have with using hip-hop as a tool for teaching. When teachers allow students to "school" the teacher on aspects of the culture, students are willing to be schooled on science. Furthermore, the teacher begins to teach from a place of understanding of students rather than a fear of them.

Teaching without fear allow for an expression of vulnerability. In one instance, a biology teacher who was admittedly not a part of hip-hop, and not initially interested in the culture, shared with students that he wanted to learn about hip-hop and how important it was to students. In response, he received so much assistance from students before and after school on planning and designing lessons and activities, that he had revamped lesson plans (with students' help) for the entire school year in three weeks. Students would suggest examples to use in the lesson, would coteach classes, and would come to the teacher's defense when classroom management issues with other students developed in the classroom. This approach to instruction is incredibly valuable and lacks such visibility in traditional science education that it is a disservice to both teachers and students.

Invisibility of Hip-hop's Insight Into Teaching and Learning

As discussed throughout this book, within urban science classrooms, oppressive structures beyond the classroom are often replicated within them. "Those empowered within dominant culture are visible, and visibility itself empowers" (Oliver, 2001, p. 108). Concurrently, invisibility and the blinding of the hip-hop participant's vision of, and into teaching is commonplace in the urban classroom.

Engaging in Reality Pedagogy reflects an awareness of the existing invisibility of hip-hop and an acknowledgment of its potential for improving the teaching of hip-hop youth. A teacher attempting to start a biology laboratory lesson on genetics in an ethnically diverse urban classroom without accounting for, or exploring students' diversity and genetic traits inherently supports a loss of voice for students whose voices are already often silenced. This reflects an ignoring of their realities. Moreover, a genetics lesson introduced in this class that does not provide students an opportunity to teach each other about their family histories, or understand how these histories relate to a specific scientific topic reflects the teacher's supporting of the invisibility of hip-hop youth. In instances where students' knowledge and histories are not given a space to be expressed, when they can so readily supplement the lesson, the classroom functions to support the students' disempowerment. Disempowerment within a particular social field is often the trigger for disinterest within that field and a cause for hyper-engagement in another field that gives a space for full participation (Dunn et al., 2003). I, for example, became more involved with hip-hop when it became a place where I could belong when I felt uncomfortable or felt uninvolved within the classrooms in my high school. This infatuation with hip-hop grew into a deep devotion when it provided me with the opportunity to express my frustration with not having a voice in school. Through hip-hop, I could talk about living in an overcrowded apartment or express my worry about the well being of my siblings. In hip-hop, I had an avenue to display my intelligence, and explore my interests, and express my vulnerabilities while building my confidence. I could write a rap with all the scientific vocabulary I had taught myself, talk about my experiences and teach whoever wanted to know more about my culture or me. I had my own approach to pedagogy.

Pedagogy, defined as the science of teaching, traditionally gets enacted in ways that are designed for a different population than hip-hop youth in urban settings. Traditional pedagogies are created for populations who have certain homogenized characteristics, exhibit certain "accepted" behaviors, and can be described as "normal" or the norm. Goffman (1967) describes "normals" as people who meet certain social criteria and have the ability to push others to the periphery. Participants in hip-hop are a population far from this norm and require particular effort in order to move their realities from the peripheral place they currently hold, to a more central part of teaching and learning.

Viewing the Classroom as a Space with its Own Reality

Searle (2005) introduces the concept of "reality" as an agreed upon outlook on or about social life based on how it is perceived or created by a group of people. He argues that reality is based on "facts relative to a system of values that we hold" (p. 15). I extend this outlook on/definition of reality to include how certain groups of people respond to an outlook of the world that lies beyond them. For participants in hip-hop, there is what rapper Talib Kweli calls a "paradox we call reality" where fairness, equity, and the provision of an avenue for voice are paramount despite the presence of violence or other negative phenomena seen in the hip-hop lifeworld (Kweli, 1999).

Reality Pedagogy considers the paradoxical realities within hip-hop by focusing on the experiences of the hip-hop participants (whether positive or negative) as a conduit through which they can connect to science. In the enactment of Reality Pedagogy for science education, practices that are not considered acceptable in conventional classrooms like shootings, stabbings, or writing graffiti are not pro-moted, but are discussed and connected to teaching. The science in the sounds of gunshots, the body's responses to a stabbing and the chemical composition of aerosol spray paint are all acceptable lessons because the concepts of reality and pedagogy converge in ways that promote learning. The amalgamation of these concepts (reality and pedagogy) is the first step towards creating an approach to the teaching of science that benefits populations who are immersed in a reality that is different from the culture of the classroom.

In order to understand reality as it relates to student experience, we must look at the classroom and view it as a unique space where a specific type of reality that is other than the students' out of school reality is created and enacted. Oftentimes, the structures within the urban science classroom seek to create a modernist reality where what occurs within it is scripted and removed from what lies right outside its walls in the students' neighborhood. In most instances, this scripted classroom involves the use of approaches to instruction that rest almost exclusively on lecture/direct instruction and does not consider anything that the students come to the classroom with. In a sense the classroom, particularly the traditional corporate classroom, is a separate world from the rest of the students' lifeworlds. While this fact about the classroom's pseudo separation from real life is often a detriment to students, I hope to make it clear that this separation from students' reality can also be a benefit if utilized appropriately by teachers. In other words, if the students are experiencing challenging real life situations outside of school that are harmful to their well being, the science class can be a place where they are temporarily shielded from these challenges while they are allowed to be themselves. For example, as an administrator in urban schools, I always urged teachers to create a classroom environment that was aesthetically pleasing- rich with posters, pictures, quotes about science that reflect the importance of science and school. While this focus on a print rich classroom environment is common practice for progressive teachers and scholars who understand the importance of a visually stimulating classroom environment (Fromberg & Bergen, 2006), I argued for an incorporation of pieces of the students' lifeworlds in the classroom. Pictures of the students, the apartment buildings where they live, profound quotes from hip-hop artists, and pictures of scientific phenomena in their neighborhoods like rocks in parks, or weathering in the surface of their apartment buildings had to be part of the classroom. These phenomena had to be merged with pictures and quotes from scientists from varying ethnic backgrounds that are side by side with pictures of students.

While I was obligated to tell teachers to follow the state curriculum, I also made it a point to tell them that our larger focus was making sure that students and teachers spoke to each other in ways that acknowledged a mutual respect for each other, and the cultures they each represent. I pushed teachers to see that every conversation between students and their teachers were tools through which they could talk about science. In the role of school administrator, I was given the oppor-tunity to create a science classroom where the students' classroom reality was one where they felt like a part of science. They walked into a classroom where they were surrounded with both their hip-hopness and science, and this was a new reality. When students walked into a beautifully decorated classroom with a teacher who teaches them science by firstly validating who they are as scholars and acknowledging that they are scientists in their own right by virtue of being hip-hop, their perceptions of reality, or at least a science class reality, can change.

Validating and Utilizing Hip-hop Students' Standpoints

Reality Pedagogy acknowledges non-dominant standpoints and the nuances of the experiences that come from these standpoints; and utilizes the position of those viewed as "Other" as the point from which pedagogy is birthed. When Reality Pedagogy is developed, rituals that are conducive to science teaching and learning are developed, and transformative teaching and research continues to nourish them. For a teacher enacting Reality Pedagogy, distinct aspects of the students' hip-hop culture are observed and used as tools for instruction. For example, the detailed exchange of batons among the speakers in a rap cypher, the reading of cues as to when to actively participate in this same social field, the ability to make sense of complex oral text (speech, rhyme) are all attributes that some participants in hip-hop possess. Reality Pedagogy uses these phenomena to guide the ways that teachers teach science or coordinate group activities in the classroom. A teacher can use tools from the cypher to determine the level of communication between student and teacher. For example, a teacher can use tools from the cypher like having cues for turns at talk rather than having hands raised when deciding who gets to talk and in what order. This can lead to a reordering of existing hierarchies within urban science classrooms where teacher culture or the culture of science is typically positioned above student culture. Furthermore, it allows instruction to begin with a consideration of the students' standpoints. By standpoint, I refer to "the social positioning of the subject of knowledge, [and] the knower and creator of knowledge" (Smith, 2005, p. 9). In the context of our discussion (enacting Reality Pedagogy), our task is to reshape existent hierarchies by positioning the hip-hop students' knowledge as the norm by valuing their standpoints. This re-positioning of standpoints in favor of the group that is traditionally considered the other is valuable in enacting pedagogy that is responsive to the needs of the marginalized.

ON COGENERATIVE DIALOGUES

Cogenerative dialogues, which were discussed earlier, and are conversations between students and teachers about the classroom, are a way for teachers to take cues about the ways that students communicate. Utilizing the insights gained from these dialogues, teachers develop tools for teaching science or conducting research more effectively. Through the enactment of cogenerative dialogues, and the insight into hip-hop and urban youth provided by this book, I intend for science educators to raise their perceptions about the influence of hip-hop on the classroom to another level. I am suggesting that through this work, hip-hop will begin to be studied with the kind of critical reflection and analysis we use to study science.

Embarking on the journey to study hip-hop more closely is facilitated by the science teacher's introduction to a more comprehensive understanding of self and increased understanding of the responsibility of an urban science educator. This urban science educator identity is one that is more inclusive of the values and cultural interests of students, less focused on pre-established perceptions of students, and more focused on leading students to success in science.

In too many cases, through their commitment to science, teachers fit themselves into a mold of who a science teacher is that forces a blanket condemnation of all phenomena that do not meet specific scientific criteria. The transition from a teacher to an urban science educator requires an awareness that the teachers' indoctrination into the world of science teaching oftentimes creates a gulf between self as cold and objective scientist and self as a more artistic humanistic being. The science teacher may be cold and objective, but the educator is appropriately subjective, and considers the students as people with thoughts and ideas that are integral to teaching. Therefore, I argue that there is a progression from the average science teacher to urban educator. And then, there is a requirement for the urban science educator to consider the complexities of hip-hop as part of instruction.

In order to move beyond being the prototypical science teacher, and into an educator that considers the effects of student experiences with prototypical teachers as they go through school, cogenerative dialogues with students about their challenges with learning in teacher and not educator led classrooms are necessary. While traditional educators may consider both Reality Pedagogy and cogenerative dialogues as approaches to science instruction that transgress necessary student and teacher boundaries, I argue that the notion of necessary boundaries between students and teachers in relation to delivering content within the science classroom, defeats the purpose of teaching.

In my work, I find that each time I enact practices that value the students' hip-hop culture, and cross boundaries into their lifeworlds during my instruction, I connect them to the classroom and to science in more profound ways than I had in previous endeavors. Furthermore, with each experience I gain by immersing myself in the students' lifeworlds, I gain more knowledge on how the students think and learn. I learn how students manoeuvre through, and overcome obstacles in life, and I understand more about their everyday rituals. With this type of insight into their lifeworlds, I can identify their personal obstacles, correlate them to academic obstacles like standardized exams or an upcoming test, and challenge students to overcome their academic obstacles just as they do their personal ones.

Immediate Benefits of Cogenerative Dialogues and Reality Pedagogy: On Analogy and Student Recommendations

Teachers who consistently supports transactions in the science classroom, and welcome students' hip-hop based examples in their lessons, will always be able to generate more creative teaching tools, and illicit more interesting student examples than their peers. For example, in one classroom I worked with, a teacher had a science lesson that focused on the sustainability of ecosystems and the resources necessary for maintaining stability within them. He mentioned ecosystems that appear unchanging over decades and how they may look the same over time while they are undergoing several changes under their surface stability. Two other teachers in the school were teaching this topic and observations of each of their classrooms uncovered that the student level of interest in the topic was very low. However, in the class where the teacher had enacted cogenerative dialogues, and enacted Reality pedagogy, students drew a number of comparisons between the topic and scenarios in their lifeworlds. One student was able to draw a comparison between the lesson and images of financial stability that commercially successful rap artists maintain while they undergo financial hardship. She talked about a famous rap artist that she used to see on television who still lives in the same housing projects that she does. Before long, this analogy was extended to include the different things that it takes to maintain a standard of living for artists compared to what it takes to maintain an ecosystem. The extension of the initial analogy between hip-hop and an ecosystem became the main driving force of the teacher's lessons and became the chief motivator for students to participate in subsequent classroom discussions on ecosystems.

The use of analogy to connect the students and their lifeworlds to science was also apparent in a chemistry class where students compared an artist's relevance to his audience with the distance between objects and the electrical force between them. This particular analogy described how the distance between a rap artist and his audience was related to the artists' "realness" or ability to be respected in the neighborhoods they come from. Other students made this same comparison between an artist's relevance and his financial success. The idea presented by the students was that the further the distance between two objects, the weaker the electrical forces between them. This observation from hip-hop developed into conversations about atoms that gained or lost electrons and artists that gained fame and lost hip-hop fans because of their commercial success. As in the previous example, this discussion sparked conversations that honed students' interests and helped the teacher to use the same analogies that students developed in their future lessons.

In this same class, a different discussion based on a polymer chemistry lesson yielded analogies that were drawn between the formation of polymers from mono-mers and the ways that rap artists "have each others back" and form larger groups or crews. When given the opportunity to extend these discussions and expand their use in the classroom, comparisons were also drawn between the bond between groups of artists or neighborhood crews and the irreversible chemical process of thermosetting. For students, thermosetting mirrored the strong bonds between members of rap groups or crews and the camaraderie developed when people "are from the same hood." In each of the instances where the validation of the complex comparisons that students made between hip-hop and science occurred, they resulted in the deep interest of their peers, their use by teachers in other classes, or oppor-tunities for teachers to either address students' scientific misconceptions or have more detailed conversations with students about the topic being discussed. In fact, I find that once analogies that involve hip-hop and rap become prevalent in the classroom, they can serve as an indicator that the teacher is engaged in a process where students' realities are a key aspect of the pedagogical approaches employed in the classroom.

On Becoming a Reality Pedagogue

Becoming a reality pedagogue not only requires an understanding of the hip-hop students' ways of knowing, but also an attentiveness to the researcher/teacher's fundamental beliefs. This involves an awareness that one's background may cause the person to view the world in a way that distorts, dismisses or under-emphasizes the positive aspects of another person's ways of knowing. This awareness of one's self is integral to the teacher/researcher's situating of self as reality pedagogue or urban science educator because an awareness of one's deficiencies is the first step towards addressing them. The teacher whose students are a part of the hip-hop generations must prepare for teaching not by focusing on the student, but focusing on self. The teacher must understand what makes her think, where the desire to be a teacher comes from, and what the role of science is in this entire process. The urban science teacher must then present this true picture of self to the student. Teachers in the urban classroom must tell students where they come from, how they were raised, why and when they began to love science, how they chose to become a science teacher, and what their previous experiences have been within the kinds of social contexts the students come from. This is necessary even if there is no familiarity with hip-hop culture or urban contexts because the hip-hop culture is so rooted in being true to oneself, or "keeping it real" that it welcomes new understandings that vary from established norms more than hip-hop identities that are duplicates of pre-existent ones. Because hip-hop is founded on the assimilation of different and distinct cultures, participants in hip-hop would accept a teacher who has no previous connection to the culture but is willing to learn about it, before it accepts one who believes that she knows what it is like to be either hip-hop or urban. This is why autobiography is such a significant tool in teaching hip-hop participants. It allows teachers to present themselves to the classroom through anecdotes and artifacts about their own lives. When the teacher can "keep it real" in this manner, the space becomes created within the classroom for students to present their own autobiographies and begin to see that it is acceptable to present one's true self in the science classroom. This process not only provides a deeper understanding of where the teacher/researcher stands, but also helps students to understand that they are just as valued as the teacher.

The vulnerability that the teacher/researcher exposes to the classroom in this process closely aligns to the ways participants in hip-hop express their innermost selves to other participants in the culture. For example, on any given rap album, the listener is given information about where the artist comes from, the struggles in the artist's life, information about the artist's family, and even the person's dreams, goals, and fantasies. By presenting the role that science has played in the teacher's life as a part of the autobiography presented to the class, the significance of the discipline becomes expressed to students and they begin to see how it may possibly stand as part of their lives. The students begin to search for opportunities to tell their own stories about how and when they began to love or interact with science and if these stories don't yet exist, they begin to search for opportunities to develop the science part of their life stories.

It is because of my value for autobiography in scholarly work, that I began this work by positioning myself as a Black man raised in the inner city who has been subject to the influence of hegemonic forces throughout my experiences in schooling. However, as I present this part of my life story, I also describe myself as a college professor who works within schools and is in a constant search for new ways for looking at the teaching of science in urban schools that meets the needs of the hip-hop generation. For my descriptions of the state of urban science education, and the ways that the field must be looked at for a generation who has been removed from it, I do not rest solely on the experiences of my youth. Nor do I speak only from my position as researcher. I chose to utilize both of these pieces of who I am, and any more that reveal themselves as I work because it is hip-hop to do so. By this, I mean that in order to "keep it real" and not just write about hip-hop without expressing my hip-hopness, my full self must be woven into the work. This "self" includes the appreciation I have developed for the traditional education structures through which I have manoeuvred, as well as my appreciation for the complexities inherent in being a part of hip-hop. Rather than abandon my varying experiences and allow them to become a deficiency, I choose to utilize them to gain multiple perspectives and more critical insight into teaching and learning.

This approach aligns with the belief that the "preferred method for human science involves description, interpretation, and self reflective critical analysis" (Van-Manen, 1990, p. 4). This approach to human science, in conjunction with the rich, thick and descriptive approaches to teaching and research in science education discussed throughout this work, provides deeper understandings of the nature of participants in a culture. It also provides keen insight into the ways that both the teacher and the learner have taught and learned in contexts beyond the school. An appreciation of the complexities of these multiple contexts is essential to gain insight into how to properly engage students within school-based learning of science, which is the goal of the urban science educator.

Pre-service teachers who I have taught often discuss the nervousness and fear that they have about entering into the science classroom as a teacher for the first time. However, they rarely understand that this feeling is similar to that of the students when they enter into a classroom that is structured differently from the hip-hop fields outside of the classroom. It is also similar to the feeling that students have when they are being introduced to a scientific topic that they have never encountered before and are expected to quickly make sense of. When the teacher's experience as a newcomer to a new social field can be understood as similar to the experience of the learner, the researcher or teacher can come to grips with his subjectivity and embrace it rather than mask it by fitting into an existent role of science teacher. By focusing on human science and the nature of human complexity that comes with using autobiography as a piece of teaching and learning, a shift from a stimulus-response, mechanistic and reductionist perspective of teaching occurs and a more inclusive, student-centred, urban science educator is born.

On Everyday Tips and Approaches

Many of the concepts discussed in this book purposefully consider more abstract, self-questioning and broad aspects of science, education, and their conjoined impact on urban science education. This is the case because, a discussion only on, or emphasizing too much on practical tools for connecting hip-hop youth to science would inevitably result in a superficial rendering of the impact of hip-hop on urban science education and an employment of a "practical tip" at the expense of fully immersing oneself into hip-hop culture. For example, a recent news story describing my research using hip-hop to connect urban youth to science featured a segment where students and the teacher rapped about topics like photosynthesis and sickle cell anemia. While the work I was doing in the school involved a focus on hip-hop in a more holistic sense, and involved working with teachers to engage in Reality Pedagogy by studying the nuances of hip-hop culture, the focus was on rapping science and the use of rapping as the means through which students are connected to science. The use of rapping science, which is one of many practical tools for engaging hip-hop youth, overshadowed the fact that through an engagement in Reality Pedagogy, a science teacher may choose to rap a science topic, or may not even rap at all. The point here is that focusing on the use of practical tips for supporting the teacher that may stem from hip-hop, without a full understanding of how to effectively teach hip-hop youth, and a discussion of the shift in thinking necessary for looking at education at large, would ultimately have only a fraction of its true impact if it is successful at all.

With the point in the previous paragraph having been made, I will now consider some of the practical tools that have emerged in my work utilizing hip-hop in science classrooms. I hope to make clear that this is neither a complete list of tools, nor a how-to manual for teachers who want to use hip-hop to teach science. This work will come in an upcoming book that explores the use of Reality Pedagogy with a bevy of practical tools that meet the needs of those within the hip-hop population. What is important to make clear here is that the practices discussed here (which have been developed by teachers who are committed to understanding the role of hip-hop in urban science education), when infused into everyday practices in the classroom, develop into rituals and become a part of the structures of the classroom, and will result in the increased science agency for participants in hip-hop.

One of the most practical approaches to student involvement that I have used is the use of the call and response model of communication in hip-hop. In this process, the teacher calls out a phrase or saying and invites students to respond with an agreed upon phrase that rhymes with the initial one. This practice conjures up the structures within the out-of-school social fields that allow students to actively communicate with each other and draws students into active engagement with the classroom. When I teach, I get the students' attention when I am transitioning from one part of the lesson to the other by shouting out a phrase like "Shall I proceed?" The students then respond by saying "Yes, indeed." After this practice is enacted, it becomes a prompt that brings the entire class to be focused on the teacher, and be prepared for the next phase of the lesson. This is one of many phrases that I take from rap songs, and that I use as a signal to shift activities during the science lesson or get the students' attention when they are distracted.

On other occasions, I have appropriated the use of the hip-hop pose used in b-boying, or a celebratory gesture that students use in hip-hop such as a salute or even a short dance as a way to quietly celebrate a successful experiment or activity in the class. After I deliver a concept to students, I ask them if they understand, and get a positive response from them, I fold my arms and give a b-boy pose in front of the class. Without inviting students to give a pose, or encouraging them to do as I do, they enact the same practices after they have been successful in a class activity. Since this practice originates in the outside-of-school hip-hop field, the teacher who enacts a b-boy pose or dance allows for a natural infusion of hip-hop culture into the classroom and allows for this phenomenon to become one of the established classroom structures.

I also recommend that teachers allow students along with their "crew" to come to the board to work on classroom problems. Since I am aware that students work and move together outside of school in a communal way, I allow group work presentations to the class to be a commonplace activity inside the class. I also allow students to sign their name and "tags" on the board, and allow their final grades on certain assignments to be the average of all their individual work. Students welcome the communal structures I infuse and become invested in the achievement of their peers. In response, they begin to teach each other science through the hip-hop communal practices they normally engage in outside of the classroom. Through this process, teaching and learning is manipulated in a way that is aligned to students' lifeworlds, and science becomes a topic of discussion outside of the classroom just as much as it is within the classroom.

In my work, I have been able to bring hip-hop students to see themselves as scientists simply by welcoming students in the classroom with the phrase "Good morning scientists" and referring to them as scientists throughout the classroom lesson and in the hallways. I also start each of my classes by asking what the students had experienced the night before or what was going on in the neighborhood. This timed activity may only take 2 minutes out of a 40 minute lesson, but sets the tone for the classroom that the students and their out of school experiences are valued in the classroom. These two-minute inquiries before the class provide the educator with specific, current culturally relevant examples and analogies that can be drawn upon in the explanation of scientific concepts.

In the description of examples in urban science classrooms, it is helpful to utilize places from the students' neighborhoods, or locations from artists that are used in rap songs, as the examples to use in class. For example, when a teacher provides an example for a student and says, one day I was walking down the street and saw a rock, it provides an example in the class but not one that is vivid or relevant enough to capture the students' attention. A pedagogy focused on what the students' realities are would change the statement for students in the Bronx by saying "I was walking down Jerome Avenue (South Bronx, New York), right by the deli shop where the guys on the corner are usually rapping and I saw a rock."

I argue that the more detail related to students' contexts and culture in examples in science problems connects them more to the subject matter.

Another successful practice that supports teaching in the classroom is playing hip-hop music at a low volume in the background while students are doing problems or in a group activity. This practice causes students to speak at low volumes so that they can hear the music and inhibits the need for strict classroom management during activities where students move a lot and are more likely to speak loudly.

The combination of these types of activities and a more focused effort to literally bring the community into the science classroom combines to create a science classroom that is not only relevant to students' lives, but also more engaging. In the following section, I outline some ways that I have been able to more literally bring the community into the science classroom.

On the Community as a Curricular Resource

One of the major themes of the discussions surrounding the connection of hip-hop to school science is the importance of reaching out to the students' community. The primary way that I have accomplished this goal has been by inviting members of the community that students respect to come to the classroom to co-teach. While these individuals may not be experts in science, their stature within the community and the wealth of knowledge they have about what is happening in the neighborhood, positions them as invaluable resources for supporting the connection of hip-hop youth to science.

In my role as a science teacher in schools, I would identify participants in hip-hop culture within the community who had jobs or interests that either directly or indirectly related to science. I would then reach out to these people, have conversations with them about their work and its relation to a science topic I would be discussing in my science class, and then invite them to come and speak to the students. Some of the invitees were graffiti artists who were experts at painting with aerosol paint, cleaners who worked with harsh chemicals, and local rap artists. Graffiti artists contributed to science lessons by discussing the chemistry of containers made of tinplated steel or aluminium used to store aerosols by the graffiti artists, the chemistry of the dyes and pigments used in their artwork, and the chemistry of solvents, such as water, alcohol, and acetone that are used to dilute active ingredients to the appropriate concentration. Rappers and producers talked about the physics of soundproof booths in studios and the recording process, and how having an education can benefit someone who is interested in the kinds of careers they had chosen. In every situation where these individuals from the school community have been given the opportunity to be a part of classroom discussions, the levels of engagement for students who are a part of hip-hop have been substantially increased when compared to other lessons.

The benefits of allowing students who are a part of hip-hop to engage in science through hip-hop and their community has been supported by the findings of a research project that focused on allowing students to create their own rap songs within a science classroom (Varelas, Becker, Luster, & Wenzel, 2002). In the

Varelas et al. study, students demonstrated increased levels of interest, ownership, and pride in their work when they were able to use rap music as part of their class work. The outcomes of this research study mirror the outcomes of research I have conducted in urban science classrooms across New York City using rap as a component of a more focused attempt to use the students' community as a tool for bringing the students' hip-hopness into the science classroom.

In addition to the above suggestions, using local papers as a resource for being up to date on neighborhood news, utilizing institutions like the local church to be an avenue for a safe place to talk with community leaders about the community, and even opting to have these types of community leaders to come out to the school and speak with students involves the community in the school in a genuine way that benefits students and blurs the lines between their in school and out of school worlds.

On "I Love Hip-hop" and Connecting Students to Science

Through my study of hip-hop in its various forms across the globe, I find that there is a bond between those who are marginalized from society that causes them to develop a collective love for hip-hop that is expressed in sub-cultures of hip-hop like rap, graffiti, dance, and spoken-word. In these sub-fields, participants become completely engulfed in the culture of a particular form of hip-hop and develop a passion for hip-hop at large that becomes poured into their interactions with those from other hip-hop fields. This love is evident in the painstaking attention to detail in scratching and blending of records, the hours taken by future music producers banging on tables to create complex rhythms, the time taken by emcees perfecting raps, and hours spent defying gravity while practicing break dance moves. This phenomenon (love, connectivity, passion) is expressed within hip-hop, because, for participants in the culture, there is no separation between hip-hop and the ways they communicate with each other in their lifeworlds.

The passion for hip-hop described by participants in the culture (often expressed by rap artists in songs) is similar to the "love of science" or feeling of belonging to a "community of scholars" (DeMichele, 2002) that is often described by scientists when they are asked about their choice of science as a profession. I argue that the passion exhibited by those invested in hip-hop for the sake of hip-hop can be expressed in science and used to develop interest and participation in science. This commonly happens if the structures in the science classroom are amended to include a value for hip-hop. By this, I mean that in their articulation of their understandings of canonical science, students who are a part of hip hop may utilize their understandings of hip-hop and hip-hop culture as tools in describing what they know about science. This allows school science to be like one of hip-hop's sub-cultures that students develop a love for. The graffiti artist can be commissioned by the teacher to create posters about the scientific phenomena taught in class, or given the responsibility to design the class bulletin board. The emcee can be invited to present a topic in front of the class or create a rap based on a specific topic, and the producer can be requested to organize the materials for a lab and arrange them in a way that gets the entire class involved. This way, the love they have for specific sub-cultures in hip-hop has the opportunity to be expressed in the science classroom.

Take Away Lessons

Through the arguments made in this book, and the descriptions of Reality Pedagogy and practical tools and approaches to connecting hip-hop to science made in this chapter, I hope to have made recommendations for each of the constituencies in urban science education that can spur on the healing of the wounds that science, and urban education have inflicted on urban hip-hop youth. The work is written for the student, the teacher, the administrator and the researcher with hopes of providing deeper insight, and changing existent practice.

For students, I hope to make clear that they need not give up their hip-hop identity or hip-hopness to find success in schools or science. Through this work I show that their hip-hopness provides such deep insight into the world of science that losing it will leave the student at a disadvantage in being successful in the discipline. The student must know that the science classroom is a place that does not always represent science as it truly is. School science is different from science and has a unique culture that is more focused on schooling than true science. While school science is a form of science that students must be successful in, their responsibility within schools is to show how menial the tasks of school are by not dismissing them, but by overcoming them and proving their intelligence or superiority to the tasks at hand by being successful at them. Lastly, hip-hop students must learn that it is part of their responsibility to introduce their teachers to the culture of hip-hop and be good brokers of the culture. Oftentimes, the teacher does not know any better about hip-hop, or how to effectively teach hip-hop youth.

For the teacher, I hope to make clear that in order to begin the process of truly connecting urban youth to science, teachers most consider the ways that they (teachers) view science, and the ways that they view science education. They must also ask themselves what the goals of science are, and what are the goals of science education as it is practiced within their classrooms. If these goals do not align, or if they both consider the goals of the discipline and the practice of teaching to be gaining a finite mass of information or to be a docile conformist in the classroom or the world, I would consider the teacher reconsider the arguments made in this book, take a critical look at self as teacher, and try to assess whether science as it is practiced within their classrooms, either reflects true science or will work to make their hip-hop students into scientists.

I suggest that teachers change the ways that they view participants in hip-hop and shift from the deficit views of hop-hop that shape common discourse. Rather than spend their effort attempting to extract students' hip-hopness from who they are, I argue that students be taught from an understanding of, and consideration of, hip-hop culture. This must be done while upholding ethical standards that consider hip-hop youth to be just as intelligent as their peers from other backgrounds. Finally, I argue that it is the teacher's responsibility to learn and understand hip-hop's ancestry and how it has led to the current state of the hip-hop generation. This understanding allows the teacher to understand that students have tremendous insight into how to best teach their peers because teaching and learning is an integral part of their history.

For the researcher, it must become clear that research in urban science education must involve a consideration of context as much as content. Conducting science education research in communities that have been historically and purposefully denied access to science has to be equally focused on who is being taught and why they have not been successful in science, as the subject being taught. It is easy to stand at the back of the classroom, take notes, and then write about what the researcher sees. This approach to research is presented purely through the lens of the researcher and cannot provide a true description of the dynamics within the classroom (which are filled with rituals that the students in the classroom have developed in response to the structures in the classroom). The type of research that urban science education researchers must engage in involves conversations with students about the ways that they choose to engage within the classroom and how their engagement in hip-hop culture affects what happens within the classroom.

On Reframing Urban Science Education

To meet the larger goal of addressing the needs of hip-hop youth in urban science classrooms, urban science education must allow for the growth of a distinct academic field aligned to, yet separate from, science education where social injustice and the unaddressed sociocultural issues that perpetuate these injustices are addressed. This reframing of urban science education is a large-scale effort that requires a push to reconstruct what is considered scientific knowledge and employ strategies that foster new approaches to pedagogy (Bybee and McInemy, 1995). In this effort, the knowledge that is named as hip-hop science is considered part of traditional science. This new and more culturally rich science curriculum is focused on the ways transactions (exchanges of ideas, culture and understandings) occur in the social lives of students and considers them in the pedagogical appro-aches employed in the classroom.

Approaching urban science education from this lens requires viewing hip-hop culture as a channel through which underachievement and disinterest in school for youth engaged in hip-hop is targeted and addressed. Through this work, I have impressed upon educators that hip-hop stands as a primary link between many students and science. Furthermore, hip-hop is culture and therefore, should be included as part of the inclusion efforts of multicultural education. Students' everyday experiences in school and in science are greatly influenced by their enactments of, and the messages received from, hip-hop. Therefore, extracting hip-hop from science education equates to purposefully disengaging students in the discipline.

This focus on hip-hop as a tool for transforming science education reform has an international scope because of the visibility and accessibility of the culture to many groups of marginalized people across the globe. In nations where there is a distinct focus on transforming curriculum to meet the needs of diverse and traditionally marginalized populations like the United States, Canada, Australia and New Zealand (Ninnes, 2002), there are large populations of people who are marginalized from conventional forms of education and science achievement. Coincidentally, these nations are among the many where there are growing numbers of people who consider themselves part of hip-hop and are "moving against the stream in time and space yet residing within the confines of the mainstream" (Condry, 2001, p. 267). In other words, they hold identities that are deeply rooted in hip-hop which are considered outside of the norm. They are operating in social fields like urban science classrooms where their true selves are never exposed and their need to be a part of the structures that define the way to teach, learn and live freely are never met.

At this point, I have led the reader to see the importance of focusing on hip-hop culture in the application of science curricula. In support for my work, many reformists and scholars that look towards reframing science teaching and learning argue (albeit through different theoretical lenses) for the infusion of student culture into the science curriculum. They argue for a focus on the modes of being and intellectual activity of the learners of science (Donnelly, 2006), the use of students' communities as a tool in the teaching of science (Barton 2001), and a focus on personal narrative in the teaching of the many socio-scientific issues that are part of the science curriculum in urban schools (Levinson, 2007). Other research points to a focus on either students' communities or discourse and the nature of their interactions that vary from school (Atwater, 1996; Barton, 1998; Lemke, 1990). Taking these points a step further, I argue that an understanding of hip-hop and its relation to science is the primary tool through which these initiatives get implemented.

This work is a means through which the education of urban youth in science classrooms is reconsidered and positively transformed. It is the revelation of the potential for greatness of hip-hop youth, an unmasking of the brilliance of a generation that has not been allowed to come to its full potential within traditional urban science classrooms, and a means through which transformative teaching and research in urban settings can begin to take effect.

GLOSSARY

B-boy/B-girl – Originally associated with break dancing, one who is associated with hip-hop, adopting and reflecting the common fashion styling, musical influences, and philosophical underpinnings commonly witnessed in public performances of hip-hop dance and music.

"The block" – Urban colloquial term synonymous with neighborhood or more specifically an urban neighborhood. Neighborhood lines in this sense are almost exclusively drawn and recognized among and by the inhabitants of the area and have little resemblance to geographically/politically-designated neighborhoods. In some instances, can refer to the "cellblock" in correctional institutions. The block can also relate to a city block. Some people sometimes include multiple city blocks, and describe it as "the block."

Break dancing – Commonly recognized as the official and original dance form of hip-hop. The style is associated with the practice of dancing over the breaks (break beats) in a musical sequence that allows for rhythmic instrumentalism.

Cogenerative Dialogue – The process of constructing a forum based on cosmopolitan ideals. In a co-generative dialogue, all participants "co-generate" (collaboratively generate) the discussions and rules of conducting the discussions, as well as the outcomes. Each participant involved in the co-generative dialogue, in accordance with philosophically cosmopolitan ideals, has equal agency or the ability to act independently and with equal influence and positioning in the dialogue.

Cosmopolitanism – Mostly resonant in progressively cosmopolitan communities, or communities that have multi-ethnic, multi-cultural factions, it is the practice of equally representing and valuing the individual and collective stake of each of the community's constituents.

Culture – Individuals united in practice, ideologies, beliefs, rituals, values, or location.

Cypher – Impromptu or planned forum where individuals dialogue or rap pre-written or improvisational, also known as "free-styled" lyrics.

DJ – Originally limited to those who practiced playing albums of popular or niche musical recording artists, the DJ is now recognized as a musical recording artist after releasing a "mixtape" on either commercial or "underground" musical circuits.

Emcee – One who delivers rhythmic spoken word over a melodic or percussive beat or musical score.

Freestyle – Commonly defined as an improvisational spoken word or rap performance, free from pre-meditation. Closely related to free-verse poetry, in that the spoke word or rap is not bound by conventions or the stylings associated with a particular form.

Getting Lite – Popular dance fad practiced among New York City adolescents. Usually performed in crews and incorporates stylings reminiscent of original break dancing and break dance crews.

Ice grill – A fashion fad commonly associated with diamond-laden mouthpieces worn over the front teeth, popularized by contemporary hip-hop/rap artists. The term has been appropriated in certain communities and extended to describe unfriendly or angry facial expressions used to show displeasure or to instill fear.

Mix tape – Initially distributed only on cassettes, this includes any media audio format where the content is preselected and sometimes styled (cut, blended and scratched) by a Disc Jockey (DJ), and played in succession. The popularity of a mix tape heightens the awareness of the selector of the mix- the DJ. Mixtapes are usually characterized by copyright infringement with DJs appropriating the musical property of other recording artists, and therefore are primarily distributed and sold illegally or "underground." Sometimes mix tapes can follow a theme (regional, local, ethnic, cultural, music, or conceptual). Mixtapes often serve as a non-standardized publicity practice, preceding the release of an album for a relatively new or highly anticipated artist.

Patois – A creolization of one or more standardized root languages usually inflected with colloquial language or locally/regionally recognized slang.

Projects – Urban and suburban public housing usually owned by city or local governments and funded by the U.S. Department of Housing and Urban Development (HUD). Originally constructed as alternative housing for population boom periods (the great migration, 1970's, etc.), the projects are commonly recognized as "low-income" housing for individuals and families earning less than 30% of the local income per capita or below the poverty level in a local neighborhood or region.

Reggaeton – Spanish language rapping originally rooted in Puerto Rico and its hip-hop cultural participants and popularized by New York Puerto Ricans, which employs the rhythmic "emcee" style of delivery over reggae melodies and rhythms.

Spanglish – Mixing English with Spanish popularized in Spanish immigrant populations in American urban centers.

Swagger – Colloquial term for an individual or collective style of dress, verbal styling, mannerism, and general body language that is often characteristic of a particular cultural or local affiliation.

Turntablist – Alternative term used reflexibly with "DJ" that characterizes the primary function of the hip-hop DJ, to play or "spin" albums/CD/wax records for public performance, often showcasing improvisational rhythmic breaks, scratching, repetition.

REFERENCES

Alexander, J. C. (2005). The meaning of social life. A cultural sociology. Oxford: Oxford University Press.

Anyon, J. (2006). Radical possibilities: Public policy, urban education, and a new social movement. New York: Routledge.

Appiah, K. A. (2006). Cosmopolitanism: Ethics in a world of strangers. New York: Norton.

Arendt, H. (1958). The human condition. Chicago: University of Chicago Press.

Atwater, M. (1996). Social constructivism: Infusion into the multicultural science education research agenda. Journal for Research in Science Teaching, 33, 821–838.

Baker, H. A. (1991). Hybridity, the rap race, and pedagogy for the 1990's. Black Music Research Journal, 11(2), 217–228.

Bakhtin, M.M. (1981) Forms of time and of the chronotope in the novel, in: M. Holquist (Ed.) The Dialogic Imagination: four essays by M. M. Bakhtin, pp. 84–258. Austin, TX, University of Texas Press.

Banfield, W. (2004). Black artist invisibility: A Black composer taking care of the souls of Black folk while losing much ground fast. Journal of Black Studies, 35, 195–209.

Barton, A. C. (1998). Teaching science with homeless children: Pedagogy, representation, and identity. Journal of Research in Science Teaching, 35, 379–394.

Barton, A. C. (2001). Science education in urban settings: Seeking new ways of praxis through critical ethnography. Journal of Research in Science Teaching, 38, 899–917.

Barton, A. C., & Yang, K. (2000). The culture of power and science education: Learning from Miguel. Journal of Research in Science Teaching, 37(8), 871–889.

Bencze, J. L. (2000). Democratic constructivist science education: Enabling egalitarian literacy and self-actualization. Journal of Curriculum Studies, 32(6), 847–865.

Boudieu, P., & Passeron, J. C. (1977). Reproduction: In education, society and culture. Beverly Hills, CA: Sage.

Bourdieu, P. (1983/1986). The forms of capital. In J. G. Richardson (Ed.), Handbook of theory and research for the sociology of education (pp. 241–258). Westport, CT: Greenwood Press.

Bourdieu, P. (1984). Distinctions: The social critique of the judgment of taste. Cambridge, MA: Harvard University Press.

Bourdieu, P. (1990). In other words: Essays towards a reflexive sociology. Oxford, UK: Polity Press.

Bourdieu, P. (1993). The field of cultural production: Essays on art and literature. Cambridge: Polity Press.

Bourdieu, P & Passeron (1977) Reproduction in Education, Society and Culture. Translated by Richard Nice. Beverly Hills: Sage

Bowles, S., & Gintis, H. (1976). Schooling in capitalist America: Educational reform and the contradictions of economic life. New York: Basic Books.

Breckenridge, C., Pollock, S., Bhabha, H., & Chakrabarty, D. (2002). Cosmopolitanism. Durham, NC: Duke University Press.

Brown, B. (2006). The politics of public discourse: Discourse, identity and African-Americans in science education. The Negro Educational Review, 56(2) 205–220.

Buddens (2007). Broken Wings Freestyle (Underground Mixtape)

Bybee, R. W., & McInemy, J. D. (1995). Science curriculum reform in the United States. In Redesigning the science curriculum. Colorado, CO: Biological Studies Curriculum Study.

Carey, S. (2001). Science education as conceptual change. Journal of Applied Developmental Psychology, 21, 13–19.

Cee Lo Green (2000). Gaining ones Definition (G.O.D). On. Common sense's*Like water for Chocolate* [CD]. New York: MCA/Universal records

50 Cent (2004). If I can't. On On *Get Rich or Die Tryin* [CD] Los Angeles: Shady/Interscope records.

Chalmers, A. F. (1976). What is this thing called science? Philadelphia: Open University Press.

REFERENCES

Coburn, J. (2005). Street science: Community knowledge and environmental health justice. Boston: M.I.T Press.

Coleman, J. (1988). Social capital in the creation of human capital. American Journal of Sociology, 94(Suppl.), s95–s120.Listed as 1998 in text. Please correct where necessary.

Comer, J. (1996). Rallying the whole village: The comer process. New York: Teachers College Press.

Common (1997). 6th sense. On *Like Water for Chocolate* [CD] New York: Geffen Records

Common (2005). It's your World. On *Be* [CD] New York: G.O.O.D/Geffen Records

Condy, I. (2002). A history of Japanese hip-hop: Street dance, club scene, pop market. In T. Mitchel (Ed.), Global noise: Rap and hip hop outside the USA (pp. -). Middletown, CT: Wesleyan University Press. Listed as Condry 2001-please correct where necessary.

Cordero, A. (2001). Scientific culture and public education. Sci & Educ, 10, 71–83.

Council of Graduate Schools. (2009). U.S. graduate education: Key to a prosperous and secure future. Retrieved May 19, 2009, from http://www.cgsnet.org/portals/0/pdf/GR_TransitionRecs.pdf

Courtlander, H. (1992). Negro folk music. New York: Dover Publishing.

Derry, G. N. (1999). What science is and how it works. Princeton University press.

D. Junk (2007). Walk it out. On. *Beat'n down yo Block* [CD] New York: Bog OOmp records, Koch records

Darling-Hammond, L. (1997). The right to learn: A blueprint for creating schools that work. San Francisco: Jossey-Bass.

Dead Prez (2000). They Schools. On *Lets Get Free* [CD] New York: Loud Records

DeMichele, J. (2002). Why scientists do science: A trek for answers. Journal of Young Investigators, 1(6) 1–6.

DiMaggio, P. (1997). Culture and cognition. Annual Review of Sociology, 23, 263–287.

Dissayanke, E. (1979). An ethological view of ritual and art in human evolutionary history. [Electronic Version]. Leonardo, Vol. 12, MIT Press, pp. 27–31.

Donnely, J. (2006). The intellectual positioning of science in the curriculum, and its relationship to reform. Journal of Curriculum Studies, 38(6), 623–640.Cited in text?

Douglas, T. (1994). Scapegoats: Transferring blame. London, UK: Routledge.

Dunn, K., Ghandi, V., Burnley, I., & Forrest, J. (2003). Racism in Australia: Cultural imperialism, disempowerment and violence. In J. Gao, R. Le Heron, & J. Logia (Eds.), Proceedings of the 22nd New Zealand geographical society conference (pp. 175–179). Auckland, New Zealand: Geographical Society Conference Series no. 22.

Emdin, C. (2009). It doesn't matter what you think. This is real. In W.-M. Roth & K. Tobin (Eds.), Reuniting psychological and sociological perspectives (pp. -). Netherlands: Springer.

Emdin, C. (2007a). Exploring the contexts of urban science classrooms. Part 2: The emergence of rituals in the learning of science. Cultural Studies of Science Education, 2, 351–392.

Emdin, C. (2007b). Exploring the contexts of urban science classrooms. Unpublished Doctoral Dissertation, The Graduate Center, City University of New York, New York.

Emdin, C. (2008). The three c's for urban science education. Phi Delta Kappan, 89(10), 772–775.

Emdin, C., & Lehner, E. (2006). Situating cogenerative dialogue in a cosmopolitan ethic. Forum Qualitative Sozialforschung/Forum: Qualitative Social Research [On-line Journal], 7(2), Art. 39. Retrieved February 3, 2007, from http://www.qualitative-research.net/fqs-texte/2-06/06-2-39-e.htm

Emdin, C., & Lehner, E. (2007). Situating cogenerative dialogue in a cosmopolitan ethic. Forum Qualitative Sozialforschung/Forum: Qualitative Social Research [On-line Journal], 7(2), Art. 39. Retrieved February 3, 2007, from http://www.qualitative-research.net/fqs-texte/2-06/06-2-39-e.htm

Fabolous (2006). In my Hood. On *Real Talk* [CD] New York: Def jam Records

Ferguson, R. F. (2001). Test score trends along racial lines, 1971–1996: Popular culture and community academic standards. In N. J. Smelser, W. J. Wilson, & F. Mitchell (Eds.), America becoming (pp. 348–390). Washington, DC: National Academy Press.

Forman, M. (2002). The hood comes first: Race, space, and place in rap and hip-hop. Middletown, CT: Wesleyan University Press.

Fraser,N. (1992). Rethinking the Public Sphere. A contribution to the critique of actually existing democracy. In C. Calhoun (Ed). Habermas and the public sphere. pp 109-142. Cambridge: MIT Press

Fromberg, D.P.,and Bergen,D. (2006). Play from Birth to 12. New York: Routledge.

Fuller, S. (2003). Philosophy, rhetoric, and the end of knowledge: The coming of science and technology studies. Madison, WI: University of Wisconsin.

Gates, H. L., Jr. (1991). Introduction. Bearing witness: Selections from African-American autobiography in the twentieth century. New York: Pantheon.

Geertz, C. (1973). *The interpretation of cultures.* New York: Basic Books.

George, N. (1999). Hip Hop America. New York: Penguin.

Goffman, E. (1967). Interaction ritual. New York: Random House.

Goffman, E. (1971). Social life as drama. In C. Lemert, & A. Branaman (Eds.), The Goffman reader (pp. 95–107). Oxford: Blackwell.

Greene, M. (1995). Releasing the imagination. San francisco: Jossey Bass.

Guba, E., & Lincoln, Y. (1989). Fourth generation evaluation. Newbury Park, CA: Sage Publications.

Haight,W. L. (2002). African American children at church: A sociocultural perspective. New York: Cambridge University Press.

Harold Melvin & The Blue Notes (1975). Wake up Everybody. On *Wake up Everybody * [CD] Philadelphia: Philadelphia International

Hayek, F. von. (1952). The counter-revolution in science. Glencoe, IL: Free Press.

Hill, M. L. (2009). *Beats, rhymes, and classroom life: Hip-hop pedagogy and the politics of identity.* New York: Teachers College Press.

Hooks, B. (2004). Rock my soul: Black people and self-esteem. New York: Atria Books.

Jasanoff, S. (1990). The fifth branch: Science advisers as policymakers. Cambridge, MA: Harvard University Press.

Jasanoff, S. (1991). Acceptable evidence in a pluralistic society. In: D. G. Mayo & R. D. Hollander (Eds), Acceptable evidence. Science and values in risk management, pp. 29–47. New York/Oxford: Oxford University Press.

Jay Electronica (2008). Something to hold on to. *What the f*ck is a Jay Electronica*[CD] Underground Mixtape

Jay-Z (1998). Hard knock life. On *Volume 2... Hard knock life * [CD] New York: Rocafella/Def jam records

Jim Jones (2005). My Diary. On *Diary of a summer* [CD] New York: E1 Music

Kane, T. J., Rockoff, J. E., & Staiger, D. O., (2006). What Does Certification Tell Us About Teacher Effectiveness? Evidence from New York City" NBER

Kennedy, C., & Kennedy, J. (1996). Teacher attitudes and change implementation. System, 20, 315–360.

Killah Priest (1990). Science Project. On *Heavy Mental* [CD] New York: Geffen Records

Kilpatrick, W. (1971). Physical science teachers grow in trees. Journal of Science Education, 55(1), 1–5.

Kincheloe, J. (1991). Teachers as researchers. Qualitative inquiry as a path to empowerment. London: The Falmer Press.

Kincheloe, J. (1999) How Do We Tell the Workers? The Socioeconomic Foundations of Work and Vocational Education. Boulder, Colo.: Westview Press.

Kincheloe, J. (2001). Getting Beyond the Facts: Teaching Social Studies/Social Science in the Twenty-First Century (2nd edition). New York: Peter Lang.

Kitwana, B. (2002). The hip-hop generation. New York: Basic Books.

Kitwana, B. (2002). The hip hop generation: Young Blacks and the crisis in African-American culture. New York: Basic/Civitas Books.

Kweli (1999). Respiration.On *Mos def and Talib Kweli are Backstar* [CD] New York: Rawkus records.

Ladson-Billings, G. J. (1995). Toward a theory of culturally relevant pedagogy. American Education Research Journal, 35, 465–496.Cited in text?

REFERENCES

Lankford, H., Loeb, S., & Wyckoff, J. (2002). Teacher sorting and the plight of urban schools: A descriptive analysis. Educational Evaluation and Policy Analysis, 24(1), 37-62.

Lau, I. C. Y., Yeung, A. S., Jin, P., & Low, R. (1998). Towards a hierarchical multidimensional English. Self Concept, 91, 747–755.

Levinson, R. (2007). Promoting the role of the personal narrative in teaching controversial socio-scientific issues. Science and Education. 17(8), 855–71.

Lemke, J. (1990). Talking science: Language learning and values. Norwood, NJ: Ablex Publishing

Lincoln, C. E. (1961). The Black muslims in America. Boston: Beacon Press

McLaren, P. (1986). Schooling as a ritual performance: Towards a political economy of educational symbols and gestures (2nd ed.). New York: Routledge.

McWhorter, J. H. (20052003 listed in text). Winning the race: Beyond the crisis in Black America. City, State: Gotham Books.

Melle-Mel (1982). The Message. On [CD single] New York: Sugar Hill records

Mitchell, T. (2001). Global noise: Rap and hip-hop outside the USA. Middletown, CT: Wesleyan University Press.

Miyakawa, F. (2005). Five percenter rap: God hop's music, message, and Black muslim mission. Bloomington, IN: Indiana University Press.Cited in text?

Montgomery, S. (2004). Of towers, walls, and fields: Perspectives on language in science. Science, 303, 1333–1335.

Mos Def (1999). Mathematics. On *Black on Both Sides* [CD] New York: Rawkus/Priority records Records

Mos Def. (2004). Sunshine. On *The New Danger* [CD] New York: Geffen Records

Nas (1994). One love. On *Illmatic* [CD] New York: Def Jam Records

Nas (2006). These are our heroes. On *Hip-hop is dead* [CD] New York: Def Jam Records

National Center for Education Statistics. (2006). Nation's report card 2005 assessment results. Washington, DC: U.S. Department of Education.

Neal, M. A. (1999). What the music said: Black popular music and Black public sphere. New York: Routledge.

Nelly (2005). Nobody Knows. On *Sweatsuit * [CD] New York: Derrty/Universal Records

Newton, D. P. (2002). Talking sense in science. City, State: Routledge Farmer.

Ninnes, P. (2002). Discursive space(s) in science curriculum materials in Canada, Australia and Aotearoa/New Zealand. Journal of Curriculum Studies, 34(5), 557–570.

New York City Department of Education, (2007). Annual School Reports, www.nycenet.edu/daa/ SchoolReports/_New York State Education Department (2007). NYC student test score data. Retrieved September 15th, 2007, from http://www.emsc.nysed.gov/ deputy/Documents/3-17-srcpressrelease-new.htm

Notorious B.I.G. (2004). Party and Bullshit. [CD single]. New York: Bad Boy/Arista records.

Oliver, K. (2001). Witnessing: Beyond recognition. Minneapolis, MN: University of Minnesota press.

Planet Asia (2000). Place of Birth. [CD single] New York: Los Angeles: ABB records

Pollock, S. (2000) 'Cosmopolitan and Vernacular in History,' Public Culture.12(3): 591–626.

Quinn, E. (2005). Nuthin' but a "G" thang: The culture and commerce of Gangsta Rap. Columbia University Press.

Ramsey, G. P. (2003). Race music: Black cultures from bebop to hip-hop. Berkely, CA: University of California Press.

Rass Kass (1997). Soul on Ice remix. [CD single] Los Angeles: Priority Records

Rhymefest (2007). Man in the mirror. On *Man in the Mirror Mixtape* [CD] Mixtape

Ridley, B. K. (2001). On science. City, State: Routledge.

Rivkin, S.,Hanushek, E., & Kain, J. (2005). Teachers, schools, and academic achievement Econometrica, 73(2), 417-458.

Rockoff, J. E. (2004). "The Impact of Individual Teachers on Student Achievement: Evidence from Panel Data." American Economic Review 94,no.2 (May):247-252.

Rodriguez, A. J. (1997). The dangerous discourse of invisibility: A critique of the national research council's national science education standards. Journal of Research in Science Teaching, 34, 19–37.

Roots. (1996). What They do.On *Illadelph Halflife* [CD] New York: Geffen records

Roscoe, (2003). Young Roscoe. On*Young Roscoe Philaphorna* [CD] New York: Los Angeles: Priority: EMI records

Rose, T. (1994). Black noise: Rap music and Black culture in contemporary America. Middletown, CT: Wesleyan University Press.

Roth, W. M., Tobin, K., & Zimmerman, A. (2002). Coteaching/cogenerative dialoguing: Learning environments research as classroom praxis. Learning Environments Research, 5, 1–28.

Rudolph, J. (2002). Scientists in the classroom: The cold war reconstruction of American science education. New York: Palgrave Macmillian.

Sapienza, A. M. (2004). Managing scientists: Leadership strategies in scientific research (2nd ed.). Hoboken, NJ: Wiley-Liss.

Scarborough, D. (1925). On the trail of Negro Folk Songs. Hatboro, PA: Folklore Associates

Schoonmaker, T. (2003). Fela: From West Africa to West Broadway. JCity, State: Acana Media.

Scott, J. C. (1990). Domination and the arts of resistance. New Haven, CT: Yale University Press.

Searle, J. (2005). The construction of social reality. New York: Free Press.

Seiler, G. (2005). All my life I been po: Oral fluency as a resource for science teaching and learning. In K. Tobin, G. Seiler, & R. Elmesky (Eds.), Improving urban science education: New roles for teachers, students, and researchers (pp. 113–130). New York: Rowman and Littlefield.Cited in text?

Sen, A. (2006). Identity and violence: The illusion of destiny. Penguin Books: London.

Sewell, W. H., Jr. (1992). A theory of structure: Duality, agency, and transformation. American Journal of Sociology, 98(1), 1–29.

Sleeter, C. (2001). Preparing teachers for culturally diverse schools: Research and the overwhelming presence of Whiteness. Journal of Teacher Education, 52(2), 94–106.

Smith, L. (1999). Decolonizing methodologies: Research and indigenous peoples. London: Zed.

Smith, D. (2005). Institutional ethnography: A sociology for people. New York: Rowman and Littlefield.

Stovall, D. (2006).Hip-hop Culture, Critical Pedagogy, and the Urban Classroom. Urban Education. (41) 6, 589-602.

Swidler, A. (1986). Culture in action: Symbols and strategies. American Sociological Review, 51(2), 273–286.

Swidler, A. (1986). Culture in Action. Symbols and Strategies. American Symbols and Strategies. American Sociological Review. 51: 273-286.

T. I. (2005). Warriors Theme.On *Warriors Theme* [CD] Atlanta: Grand Hustle/Arista records.

Tate, W. (2001). Science education as a civil right: Urban schools and opportunity-to-learn considerations. Journal of Research in Science Teaching, 38(9), 1015–1028.

Tobin, K., & Roth, W. M. (2005). Coteaching/cogenerative dialoguing in an urban science teacher preparation program. In W. M. Roth & K. Tobin (Eds.), Teaching together, learning together (pp. 59–77). New York: Peter Lang.

Tupac (1998). Changes. On *Tupac Greatest Hits * [CD] New York: Death Row/Interscope records.

Turner, J. H. (2002). Face to face: Toward a sociological theory of interpersonal behavior. Stanford, CA: Stanford University Press.

Tyack, D., & Cuban, L. (1995). Tinkering toward utopia: A century of public school reform. Boston: Harvard Univ. Press.

U.N.E.S.C.O. (2004). Science education in danger. Retrieved May 18, 2009, from http://unesdoc.unesco. org/images/0013/001368/136850e.pdf

U.S. Census. (2008). An older and more diverse nation by midcentury. Retrieved May 19, 2009, from http://www.census.gov/Press-Release/www/releases/archives/population/012496.html

U.S.D.O.E. (2009). http://idea.ed.gov/

U.S. Information Agency, Office of Research and Analysis. (1959). Impact of U.S. and Soviet space programs on world opinion. U.S. President's Committee on Information Activities Abroad (Sprague

REFERENCES

Committee) Records, 1959–1961, Box 6, A83-10, Dwight D. Eisenhower Library, Abilene, Kansas.Cited in text?

Van-Manen, M. (1990). Researching lived experience: Human science for an action sensitive pedagogy. Albany, NY: State University of New York Press.

Varela, F. (1999). Ethical know-how: Action, wisdom, and cognition. Stanford, CA: Stanford University Press.

Varelas, M., Becker, J., Luster, B., & Wenzel, S. (2002). When genres meet: Inquiry into a sixth-grade urban science class. Journal of research in science teaching, 39(7), 579–605.

Watkins, S. C. (2005). Hip hop matters: Politics, pop culture, and the struggle for the soul of a movement. Boston: Beacon Press.

Webber, T.L. (1978). Deep like the Rivers: Education in the slave quarter community (1831-1865). New York: Norton press

West, K. (2007). West, K. (2004).Good Morning. On *Graduation * [CD] New York: Rocafella/Def Jam records.

Williams, P. (1991). The alchemy of race and rights. Cambridge: Harvard University Press.

Wilson, S. (2003). Information arts: Intersections of art, science and technology. Cambridge, MA: MIT Press.

Printed in the United States
By Bookmasters